Why Duck
How food impacts diplomacy and human relations.
Revelations of Chinese characteristics

食物如何影響外交和人際關係。
中國特色的啟示.

By
Denis G. Antoine PhD
丹尼斯・安托万博士著
Former Ambassador of Grenada
to the People's Republic of China

Table of contents
目录

Acknowledgments

I wish to acknowledge with special thanks the support of all my diplomatic colleagues with whom I served while stationed in China; particularly those who graciously shared their time while dining and listening to me speak about writing 'Why Duck'. Their demonstrated interest in this subject contributed to making this publication possible. Special mention is made about dining in Hong Kong, when a joke about duck was shared during dinner. That joke further motivated my writing. My gratitude to Miss Ma Lan, Secretary to the Embassy of Grenada in China, for her translation and edits.

I thank my friends and associates who smiled at me, for the inspiration, when I mentioned that I would write 'Why Duck'. To the duck carvers at the duck establishments and restaurants where I dined in Beijing, Dalian and other locations in China, Hong Kong and other countries where I enjoyed the service while dining. I thank all the impressive servers and waiters for their hospitable service and allowing me to take pictures. Singular mention is of my colleague and distinguished friend Antonia Hugh, Ambassador of Jamaica to China for recommending Yu Hui Guo then a student at Carnegie High School CA., USA. The valuable research conducted by Yu Hui Guo during his internship at the Embassy of Grenada in Beijing in the summer of 2017 richly informed this book. I offer my gratefulness to Ambassador David WU, for sharing his knowledge about Chinese cuisine. I offer my appreciation to my friend Ziying Jia for his friendship and guidance to some of the best duck establishments in China.

鸣谢

作者特别感谢在其驻中国期间与其一同工作的所有外交同事们的支持。尤其是那些在共进晚餐时倾听他讲述"为什么食鸭"的友善的同事们。他们对这一主题表现出的浓厚兴趣使这本出版物成为可能。值得一提的是，在香港用餐时大家分享了一则关于鸭子的笑话，那个笑话进一步激发了作者的写作灵感。另外作者也感谢格林纳达驻华大使馆大使秘书马兰，感谢她对这本书的翻译和编辑工作。

作者感谢其朋友和同事，当他提到他将写《为什么食鸭》时，同事和朋友们总是微笑鼓励他。他也感谢那些他在中国北京、大连、香港以及其他城市和其他国家的各种烤鸭餐厅用餐时为其提供服务的烤鸭师傅们。同时也感谢那些出色的餐厅服务员，感谢他们的热情服务，允许他用手机拍照。作者特别要感谢的是其朋友牙买加驻中国大使安东尼亚·休，他推荐了当时还是美国加利福尼亚州卡内基高中的学生郭昱辉。郭昱辉在2017年夏天在格林纳达驻北京大使馆实习期间进行的有价值的研究充实了这本书。作者感谢其朋友贾子颖推荐了中国的一些很好的烤鸭餐厅。

Forward
By
Ambassador Dr. Alvin Schonfeld

序言
阿尔文 • 斯克恩菲尔德

"The destiny of nations depends on how they nourish themselves," said Jean Brillat-Savarin, an 18th-century food critic. Long before the inception of the modern nation state in the 17th century, food played an essential road in diplomacy. Control and access to food and other natural resources are essential to human survival. Food also ties into political and economic development. And as far back as recorded in biblical history, we remember the words, *"I was hungry and you gave me food, I was thirsty and you gave me drink, I was a stranger and you welcomed me."* (Matthew 25:31-40).

18 世纪的美食评论家让 • 布里拉 • 萨瓦兰说："国家的命运取决于他们如何养活自己"。早在 17 世纪现代民族国家诞生之前，食物就在外交中扮演了重要的角色。对食物和其他自然资源的控制和获取对人类的生存至关重要。食物也与政治和经济发展息息相关。 早在《圣经》的记载中，就有这样的话："我饿时，你给了我食物；我渴时，你给了我水喝；我在异乡时，你收留了我"。(马太福音25：31-40）

Food diplomacy refers to a country's reliance on food resources to influence political and economical relations beyond the food industry. In modern times we remember, during a 2018 meeting in the Trump presidency with North Korea Kim Jong-Un and South Korean President Moon Jae-In a flat sea fish from Busan was used to remind Mr. Moon of his hometown port city. Also served, however, was Swiss Rosti to remind Mr. Kim of the years he was said to have spent in Switzerland.

饮食外交指的是一个国家依靠食品资源来影响食品行业以外的政治和经济关系。2018 年，在特朗普总统与朝鲜总统金正恩和韩国总统文在寅的会晤中，就有一道菜是釜山的扁海鱼，以唤起文在寅先生对他的家乡港口城市的回忆。还有一道菜是瑞士炸土豆饼，以唤起金正恩先生据说在瑞士度过的那些年的回忆。"

Again, during, the Trump presidency, French President Emmanuel Macron was served a State dinner with French food. All of this serves to ensure the guest is comfortable and make negotiations between nations more relaxed. That is not to say that attempts at a favorable response to food diplomacy "always goes as planned." In 1992 President George H. W. Bush went to Japan, during the State dinner, between the second course of raw salmon and caviar and the third course of grilled beef with a pepper sauce, he made history by becoming the first sitting American President to vomit on the Prime Minister of Japan.

再如，在特朗普总统任期内，法国总统马克龙受到了一次法国美食国宴款待。所有这些旨在让宾客放松，使国家之间的谈判更加轻松。但也并不是所有对饮食外交的尝试都能带来积极的效果。1992 年，布什总统赴日本访问，国宴中，在其吃第二道菜生三文鱼和鱼子酱以及第三道辣椒酱烤牛肉的时候，他创造了历史，成为第一位向日本首相呕吐的总统。

In this book Ambassador Denis Antoine, who served as Grenada's Ambassador to the United Nations, United States of America and the People's Republic of China, gives readers 'a taste' of life as a diplomat. He uses his broad experience and knowledge of food diplomacy to discuss his experiences in China. Such foods as Peking duck or roast duck, and Yang Chow fried rice are staples of Chinese food used in diplomacy. The book discusses the customs, styles and characteristics revealed by Chinese nationals in the preparation, service and significance of Chinese food.

在接下来的书中，曾担任格林纳达驻联合国、美国和中华人民共和国大使的丹尼斯-安托万阁下会让读者也"品"一下外交官的生活，他利用自己在饮食外交方面的广泛经验跟大家分享他在中国的经历。诸如北京烤鸭、扬州炒饭等食物都是外事宴席中常有的主食。在本书中，安托万大使还将深入探讨中国人在准备和提供美食服务方面的习俗、风格和特点，以及美食的意义。

Chapter 1
Diplomacy and dining

第一章 饮食与外交

In Beijing and the Capitals of many other large provinces of China what one sees, especially foreign eyes, are layers of a complex mixture of history and culture, mingled among tradition, commerce, and modernity. 5,000 years of civilization is being unveiled for the eyes of the modern world to see. I can't help but wonder if what is seen is a future that was envisioned. Yet, one must ask of the future imagined by whom? There are so many surprises! The prevailing question is: Why should one be amazed? The answer: China remains a civilization filled with so much charm, preserved and propelled into the new millennium.

在北京和中国许多其他大省会城市，尤其是在外国人的眼中，可以看到的是复杂的历史和文化层层叠叠，交织着传统、商业和现代元素。五千年的文明展现在现代人眼中让人不禁在想，是否我们所看到的就是曾经设想的未来。然而却又不得不问，这未来是由谁设想的。因为这里有着太多的惊喜，让人惊叹中国这个依然充满魅力的文明，是如何保存并推进到新千年的。

Gastronomy in China makes possible amazing relationships between and among leaders of provinces, organizations, families, friends, and foreign visitors, with surprising revelations about unique aspects of the culture. Gastronomy promotes effective diplomatic relations among foreign diplomats in China, especially between and among foreign diplomats and government officials. There are creative, innovative, and astonishing feats derived from the diverse features of Chinese cuisine, which reveal a most unique but common tendency of the citizens. I never could have imagined it was possible to have such intimate and vivid insight into the characteristics of a people, such as I have had, by participating and witnessing how Chinese officials and citizens conduct themselves during mealtime. What they eat, the preparation and utilization of their food culture is incredibly special. It is a pleasure to admire the etiquette and graceful customs displayed in the way most Chinese interact with each other and their guests at mealtime.

中国的美食为省级领导人、组织、家庭、朋友和外国游客之间提供了令人惊叹的人际关系，揭示了文化独特之处。美食促进了中国外交官员之间的有效外交关系，尤其是外交官员和政府官员之间。中国美食的多样特色催生了创新和令人惊叹的成就，揭示了市民最独特但又普遍的倾向。我从未想过通过参与和见证中国官员和市民在用餐时的行为举止，能够对一个民族的特点有如此亲密而生动的了解。他们吃什么，以及他们对食物文化的准备和利用都是非常特别的。欣赏大多数中国人在用餐时与彼此及招待客人互动时展示的礼仪和优雅习俗，实在是一种愉悦。

The meal setting evolves into a large extended family gathering. What becomes illuminating to observe is their common courtesies when they dine. Food is given reverence and the diners give singular attention to each other with thoughtfulness and subtlety.

在中国，吃饭的环境演变成了一个大型家庭聚会，观察一下你就会发现，他们的用餐礼节是很有意义的。食物被赋予了崇高的地位，食客们对彼此给予了体贴入微的关注。

It was interesting to learn that a common greeting among citizens in some parts of China is: (NI CHI FAN LE MA), (Have you had a meal?) I was impressed by this most caring and meaningful expression.

中国人在见面时的问候也很有意思，他们会问："你吃饭了吗?"我对这种表达方式印象很深刻，我觉得这是一种很有意义的关怀。

What is exposed about eating and foods goes beyond sustenance and requires careful attention. I am talking about what my foreign eyes see when I catch sight of Chinese distinctiveness. The opportunity to endorse the enlightening luxury expressed is not about money and nice foods alone that may have jumped to your mind. I am conveying the extravagance of the privilege to meet so many personalities with whom I interacted during meals throughout my time living and working in China. I have had the occasion to meet and intermingle with wonderfully complex people. Each Chinese citizen I met helped to enrich my views; not just about personalities, but about the attention paid to values and customs. I say people because while in China, surrounded by Chinese, I encountered a civilization of diverse ethnicities but as one people. Regardless of how many Chinese nationals there are, there is exclusivity in each one. Wherever there were similarities, a kind of harmonious flow demonstrates dutiful coexistence.

在中国，食物的意义已经远远超出了维持生计的范畴，在身为外国人的我眼里，我看到的是中国的特色。感受美食的机会，是富有启发性的一种享受，这种享受无关金钱，也无关你脑海中浮现的所有好吃的东西，而是就餐中的一种被特别优待的荣幸，这种感受来源于我在中国生活和工作时和不同的人用餐时的体验。这使我有机会与一个奇妙的复杂的民族相遇。我遇到的每一个中国人，他们的性格特点以及他们对价值观和习俗的关注，都帮助我丰富了我的观点。不管遇到多少中国人，我始终觉得每个人都很独特，但又有相似之处，一种和谐的流动展示了敬业共存的特性。

The interest shown in foreigners provides an opportunity for a great deal of learning and intrigue about the communities in China I have had the pleasure to visit while posted there. An exceptional aspect in my engagement with Chinese people derived from my discovery that, in general, there is a great deal of open-mindedness and curiosity about strangers in many communities, with a generally welcoming environment.

Coming from a "Western" orientation, I found that the average person I met in China had a vast capacity and quest to gain more knowledge of the outside world o. There was a readiness to ask questions and an eagerness to learn. While I do not claim to have a thorough knowledge of the country, nevertheless, except for the diverse nationalities clustered in major cities like Beijing and Shanghai, the growing openness the deepening reach into global affairs; and the international presence in a number of megacities in China; it is clear there is a thirst among the people to learn about what's happening outside China.

中国人对外国人表现出来的兴趣，给了我能更加了解他们的机会，也激起了我的好奇心。在与中国人接触的过程中，我发现大多数中国人对陌生人有很强的开放意识和好奇心，这为外国人营造了非常受欢迎的环境。

来自西方的我发现，在中国，很多普通人都很想加深对于中国以外的世界的了解。他们乐于提出问题，求知若渴。虽然我并不敢声称对整个中国有多透彻的了解，但是，随着聚集在北京和上海等主要城市的不同国家的人越来越多，随着中国的日益开放，中国对全球事务的深入接触，很明显，中国人比过去更渴望了解中国以外的地方发生的事情。

However, what is quite notable is the great pride in the country demonstrated by Chinese nationals and the extensive knowledge that the citizens convey about the all-encompassing history of revolution and evolution of their country. The people I met when I traveled throughout the country exhibited growing confidence in their abilities and in the government. I encountered people full of inquisitiveness with a strong desire to affirm their strength and contribution to the world. I admire the way the people are driven to validate their merit; and the growing pride in their productivity and creativity.

I appreciate their love for legendary colorful natural beauty; the symmetrical display of objects with cultural value and enhanced natural attractions and the historic gardens, hedges, landscapes, and temples that are well recorded. These characteristics are reflected in the arrangement and presentation of dishes that come to the table and the feast-like atmosphere in cultural centers. The endless social and cultural heritage, the modern performances and theatrical feats will continue to contribute to China's impact on humanity, for centuries. The diverse artistic, architectural, and anthropological treasures shared with the world for the last 5,000 years place China at the pinnacle of our world heritage. Feasting on Chinese food ranks high universally.

当然最值得注意的还是中国人表现出来的对国家的强烈的自豪感，以及中国人对中华人民共和国革命和演变历史的全面了解和广泛传播。我在中国各地旅行时遇到很多人，他们都对自己的能力和执政政府表现出越来越大的信心。我看到了一个充满好奇心的民族，他们有着强烈的愿望，愿意展示他们的能力，为世界做出贡献。

我很欣赏这个民族为验证自己的能力而不断努力的样子，也很欣赏他们对其生产力和创造力日渐增长的成就感。我欣赏他们对传奇的自然美的热爱。他们对称地展示物品，使其极具文化价值和自然吸引力。这也体现在他们的花园、树篱、绿化景观和寺庙等历史建筑中。这些特点也很好地反映在餐桌菜肴的摆盘以及饮食氛围中。中国悠久的社会和文化遗产，以及现代的表演和戏剧盛宴，都将继续促进中国对整个人类的影响，这种影响也将持续数个世纪。中国过去五千年来与世界分享的各种艺术、建筑和人类学宝藏，都使中国处于世界遗产的顶峰，同时中国美食也同样享誉全球。

Traveling through China brings one face to face with many wonderful people, and there is no easy task to simplify the complexity of the cultural experiences. However, what stands out and has moved me to share the manifestations, are the moments when I had the privilege to sit and have a meal in different communities and homes; and enjoy family traditions. I recall being welcomed to Guizhou China; it's an unforgettable visit that reminded me of when I was greeted into Ochobo, Nigeria where libation was lavish in respect for the spirit of the ancestors. In Guizhou it was a lively welcome for honored visitors, and the lavish pouring of the spirits "baijiu" was a show of gladness.

在中国旅行可以遇见许多优秀的人，要简化这复杂的文化体验可不是一件容易的事。让我觉得印象尤为深刻的就是我有幸在不同的家庭中坐下来和大家一起吃饭，一起感受特别的家庭传统，这些时刻总是让我很感动，忍不住想与大家分享我的所见所闻所感。我记得去贵州的那次访问，很令人难忘，我在中国贵州受到了热烈的欢迎，这使我想起在尼日利亚奥乔博受到欢迎的情景，那里的奠酒是对祖先精神的慷慨致敬。在贵州，对"白酒"慷慨的倾倒则表达了迎接尊贵客人到访的喜悦之情。

On arrival, visitors are bathed with the rich spirits in the tradition of the elders by glamorous ushers, as if to awaken the ancestors. The greeters in Guizhou are wrapped with beautiful costumes, in a most seductive display of the beauty of its proud, productive people. Come in, drink and be among us, are the sentiments portrayed with open arms and cups filled with the most popular alcoholic beverage Maotai, and Baijiu wines, served with unforgettable hugs and pouring of other beverages. Such servings of the spirits are presented, like clearing of the pallet before the sumptuous meal often served to strangers. When visitors are invited to dine, they are welcomed to a feast that begins with lovely, decorated tables; while guests are wooed with juicy appetizers and the best sauces from local family kitchens mixed with ingredients to provoke anyone's appetite.

抵达时，访客会在令人艳羡的引导下，在仿佛为唤醒先辈的传统仪式上，沐浴于浓郁的美酒之中。贵州的迎宾者身披美丽的服饰，骄傲地展示其引人注目之美。"请进，尽情品味，与我们共聚"，这是敞开双臂、酒杯中装满最受欢迎的茅台和白酒的情感，伴随着难以忘怀的拥抱和其他饮品的倾倒。这样的美酒款待，宛如为陌生人奉上丰盛餐前的清口之礼。当访客受邀共进晚餐时，他们将迎来一场盛宴，这盛宴以精美装饰的餐桌开始；而美味的开胃菜和来自当地家庭厨房的最佳酱料，则会让宾客沉醉其中，食欲大大提升。

Whether one likes eating duck or not, this versatile selection will be on the menu as an irresistible main course meat. There is something special surrounding the preparation and service of this bird that is an ancient secret, and quite revealing. By careful observation and scrutiny, an opening China reveals polite sentiments that date back centuries and currently manifested among its people. This is not related to the intangible heritage secret concealed in the preparation of roast duck, but that which can be identified in the way Chinese people are with each other; characteristics that have nothing to do with physiognomies and politics. What can be found answering to 'why duck' is about orientation and disposition of a people.

These revelations of a civilization that are conveyed when speaking about roast duck, are not like the saying 'Throwing water on a duck's back'. It is more like admiring how a white duck swims; therefore, it is also safe to say because a duck cleanses from within while wading. This is a partial answer to why duck dining reveals so many characteristics of Chinese people. And it could be because the society is evolving after so many centuries, and still maintains the secrets of authenticity.

无论你是否喜欢吃鸭肉，万能的鸭肉总会出现在菜单上，作为主菜，它总是让人无法抗拒。如何准备鸭肉，如何上菜也有其特别之处，颇具启示性。通过仔细观察，你会发现在当今开放的中国，仍然有着那可以追溯到几个世纪以前的中国人的儒雅。这并非体现在烤鸭制作过程中蕴含的非物质遗产的秘密里，而是从中国人彼此之间的相处方式和他们的特点中可以得见，这与人的相貌和政治都无关。那为什么食鸭？可以回答的或许是一种民族的取向和性格吧。

谈到烤鸭传达出来的这些文明的启示，不同于俗语"水滑鸭背"那么浅显，更像是欣赏一只白鸭自在的游动；因此，也可以说，因为鸭子在游动时从内部净化自己。这在某种程度上解释了为什么鸭子的用餐习惯能够揭示出中国人的许多特征。或许是因为经过了数个世纪，这个社会仍然保留着真实性的秘密，而又在不断演变。

When people travel, memories are created. I can attest to the fact that traveling in China, one soon finds endless chances to be engulfed in numerous encounters that become permanent memories. Food memories from China are impressions that linger with visitors. While the cultural expressions are unforgettable, when local people invite overseas people to social events and visitors are accommodated to dine with them in their domains, the experience is transformational. An invitation to come and have a meal provides an opportunity to see people, how they form themselves and the way they truly are. Therefore, how does the cuisine help to define Chinese people, and why do the preparation and serving of a duck feast provide a most vivid mirror to catch a reflection of some very subtle characteristics? How are the qualities of pride, courage and adventure manifested in the cuisine? These queries can be answered, by paying close attention to the routine for preparing roast duck, how it is presented at a feast and how these secrets are preserved for centuries.

当人们在旅行的时候，记忆便开始构筑。我的经历可以证明：在中国旅行，你会很快就发现有太多的机会你会沉浸在无数次的邂逅中，而这些回忆会一直留在你心中。我相信对中国美食的回忆一定是萦绕在所有游客心中的印象之一。而且中国人的文化表达方式也令人难忘，当他们邀请你去他们的地方一起用餐时，这会是让你彻底改变的经历。受邀共同进餐是个很好的可以了解对方的机会。因此，烹饪是如何帮助定义中国人的？为什么准备和供应烤鸭提供了一面最生动的镜子，可以从中捕捉到一些微妙的特质？ 中国美食是如何呈现出中国人的自豪感，勇气和冒险的品质？这些问题可以通过仔细观察中国人为宴会准备烤鸭的程序，以及烤鸭的呈现方式中窥探一二。

The table is set for a Chinese family dinner with foreign friends in Shandong near Mountain Tai (Tai Shan)
（照片由丹尼斯·安托万拍摄）
图为在山东泰山附近与中国朋友的家庭聚餐

The influence of food in ancient and modern societies has been documented in numerous early aspects of life, particularly involving diplomacy. Food is discussed extensively today on the Internet and multiple books and articles.

食物在古代和现代社会的影响已被记录在包括外交在内的生活的方方面面。现如今食物在互联网和许多书籍和文章中也被广泛的讨论。

As discussed in "Wikipedia, the free encyclopedia" and as I have observed during my own experience living in China; cuisine is an important part of culture and includes cuisines originating from China. Due to the rising number of Chinese living abroad, along with the historical strength of the country, Chinese cuisine has influenced many other cuisines in Asia and beyond; with modifications made to cater to local palates. Staple foods of China such as rice, soy, noodles, tea, chili oil and tofu; and utensils like chopsticks and the wok are found worldwide.

The preferences for seasoning and cooking techniques within the provinces of China depend on historical background and ethnic groups. The geographic features including mountains, rivers, forests, and deserts, have a strong impact on locally available ingredients. Moreover, the climate varies from tropical in the south to subarctic in the northeast. Imperial royal and noble preferences also play a role in the change of Chinese cuisine. Imperial expansion and trading have seen ingredients and cooking techniques from other cultures integrated into Chinese cuisines over time.

It is not surprising that some of the best Japanese dishes are excellently prepared by Chinese chefs in Beijing, Shanghai, and other big cities.

正如"维基百科，自由的百科全书"中所说的那样，"中餐是中国文化的一个重要组成部分"，我在中国生活的经历中感受到的也确实如此。由于现在居住在海外的中国人越来越多，以及中国的悠久历史，中国菜已经影响了亚洲和其他地区的许多其他菜系，并为迎合当地人的口味进行了调整。如今在世界各地都可以找到中国的食物，如大米、大豆、面条、茶叶、辣椒油和豆腐，也可以很容易找到筷子和炒锅等餐具。

中国各省的调味和烹饪技巧的偏好取决于历史背景和不同的民族群体之间的差异。地理特征，包括山脉、河流、森林和沙漠，也对当地的可用食材产生强烈影响。还必须考虑到中国的气候从南部的热带气候到东北部的亚寒带气候都存在差异。皇室和贵族的喜好也影响着中国烹饪的变化史。由于帝国的扩张和贸易，随着时间的推移，来自其他文化的食材和烹饪技巧被融入到中国烹饪中也是不足为奇的。因此，在中国的北京、上海和其他大城市中，中国厨师精心制作出了一些最美味的日本菜肴也就再正常不过了。

There are numerous regional, religious, and ethnic styles of cuisine found within China, as there are abroad. The most praised Four Great Traditions in Chinese cuisine are Chuan, Lu, Yue and Huaiyang, representing cuisines of West, North, South and East China, respectively.

Twenty-three years into the twenty-first century, there is a proliferation of foods. Even in societies where there are serious pockets of abject poverty, the food industry still seems to flourish. Food is an industry that pays. And food in modern Chinese societies is taking consumers "beyond their imagination" as is commonly said in Barbados. Whatever food that one can imagine is available in China and the industry promises what's not imagined is coming soon!

From fast foods and health foods to super foods, there is even space foods. Visitors to China will remain impressed by the colorful quality and the extents to which the production, preparation, distribution, making, and marketing are moving to please consumers. Food has become accessible and affordable to all classes and sectors of the population. There are even synthetic foods, while research for more dimensions of foods continues.

中国境内和海外都有众多不同地区、宗教和民族风味的中国菜。中国美食中最受赞誉的四大菜系是川菜、鲁菜、粤菜和淮扬菜，分别代表了中国的西部、北部、南部和东部的烹饪风格。

进入21世纪的22年中，各种食品在各个社会中都呈现出蓬勃的发展，即使在一些地方仍存在严重贫困的情况，但食品行业似乎仍然兴旺。食品产业是一个有利可图的行业。在现代中国社会，食品将消费者带入了"他们的想象之外"，就像巴巴多斯人所说的那样，在中国，无论你能想象到的食物是什么，都可以找得到，食品行业总是会很快提供超乎你想象的新产品。

从快餐、健康食品到超级食品，甚至现在还有太空食品，前来中国的游客们会一直被食品的质量所打动，另外食品的生产、制备、分发、和市场营销所采取的方式，都旨在取悦消费者。食品已经变得对所有阶层和人群都具备可及性和经济性。甚至现在还有合成食品，对食品的多维度研究也仍在进行中。

The use of food beyond its needs in the human body for providing nourishment focuses attention on the power of food. Food is known to be a catalyst for peace, for war. Foods to redeem social ills, such as food for the poor; sustenance for displaced people, sports diet, and so much more about food can be counted. Look at how food bombards the media and the food channels, and the busy food courts at malls and shopping centers.

对食物的食用已经不仅仅是为了满足人体营养需求，而是开始让人们重新关注食物的力量。食物可以用于解决社会问题，如为穷人和流离失所的人们提供食物等等，关于食物的用途数不胜数。食物的宣传充斥着媒体和美食频道，以及购物中心和商场的美食广场。

Sources of foods are no more confined to the traditional family farms, community gardens, green houses, and barns. In the twenty-first century, in addition to imports, many foods are coming from the laboratory. Even when foods come from apparent traditional sources, certain kinds may be genetically modified when modern cell culture is applied. As stated on Microsoft Bing Search, today there are cultured meat products; in China one can eat "Just Eggs" made from "Mung Bean," a bean that has been used for more than 5,000 years in China. Really good eggs, from plants, are also produced.

A Food Ingredients first report by Benjamin Ferrer; states. "Today Mung beans, the key ingredient for JUST Egg, are already a dietary and agricultural staple in China, and other parts of Asia. The production of the plant-based egg requires 70 percent less surface and groundwater and has a 40 percent lower carbon footprint than chicken egg production, the start-up highlights. China produces about 435 billion eggs per year and demand for protein is increasing. The company notes that urbanization, population growth, and higher incomes are accelerating such demand, yet available arable land is diminishing."

同样显而易见且有趣的是，食物的来源不再局限于传统的家庭农场、社区菜园、温室和谷仓。在 21 世纪，除了进口之外，许多食品都来自实验室。即使食品来自表面上的传统来源，某些种类也可能是转基因的，并且应用了现代细胞培养技术。正如微软必应搜索中所写："现在已经有了人工肉类制品，在中国，人们现在可以吃到由绿豆制成的蛋派，这种豆子在中国已经使用了五千多年。真正的好鸡蛋，是从植物中产生的。"如今，绿豆，即蛋派的关键成分，在中国和亚洲其他地区已经成为了一种饮食主食。新兴的生产植物性鸡蛋的公司强调指出，生产植物性鸡蛋所需的地表水和地下水可减少70%，碳排放比鸡蛋生产低40%，中国每年生产约

4350 亿枚鸡蛋，对蛋白质的需求还在持续增加。该公司指出，城市化、人口增长和收入提高正在加速这种需求，然而可用的耕地正在减少。

Today food preparation takes focus on reducing energy and water consumption as applied to production. There is welcome discussion about strengthening policy in quality and safety of foods. Yet, the increased demand for food speeds up, as the modern clusters of the world's population congregate in mega cities. It is, however, amazing to see the rich availability of foods in these modern cities.

如今，食品制备侧重减少能源和水资源的使用。在中国，对食品质量和食品安全方面的讨论和政策强化备受欢迎。然而，随着世界各地的现代人口聚集在超大城市中，对食品的需求不断增加。不过，在中国现代城市，食物的丰富供应还是令人惊叹。

As the global consensus on food emerges from the international discourse on access and food safety, policy makers, government agencies and many non-governmental organizations are using the word 'food' almost as a slogan for caring. The United Nations has a standard-bearer organization to engage in the fight against poverty; "The World Food Program." enters conflict areas, refugee camps and other hunger zones to bring food. Volumes have been written and dramatic actions are taken every day in trade shows and food fairs, with foods. Even in the practice of diplomacy and foreign relations, food becomes a leading attraction. The concept of Culinary Diplomacy and the impact of gastronomy are well documented and utilized in state policy.

随着全球对食品的共识从国际讨论中涌现出来，政策制定者、政府机构以及许多非政府组织现在几乎将食品当作关爱的标语。联合国设立了一个标杆组织来参与扶贫工作，即"世界粮食计划署"，它进入冲突地区、难民营和其他贫困地区提供食品。在贸易展会、美食博览会以及外交关系实践中，食品都成为了一个主要的吸引点。烹饪外交的概念以及美食的影响在国家政策中得到了充分记录并得到了应用。

In revolutionary history around the world, in biblical annals and in modern day, the practice of gathering food for charity is a relevant form of correcting social ills and is used to fight against scarceness of food as demonstrated in China. Note the United Nations Sustainable Development Goal #2 – "End hunger, achieve food security and improved nutrition and promote sustainable agriculture." This goal places food in a multi-dimensional function in a global sense. So, when we begin to talk about agriculture, how about duck? Ducks are already kept in the barnyard, and rearing ducks is indeed a profitable form of poultry farming in China. Duck meat is quite relevant, as it is significantly affordable and a healthy source of protein. I also read in the bible in the book of Ruth, food shortage and famine impacted the community and that had impact on behaviors.

在世界各地的革命历史中，在《圣经》中，甚至在现代，慈善募集食物的做法被视为一种纠正社会弊端、抗击粮食短缺的有效手段，这一点在中国得到了证明。联合国可持续发展第二项目标"消除饥饿，实现粮食安全，改善营养和推进可持续农业发展"将食物赋予了全球意义上的多维功能。因此，当我们开始谈论农业时，不如先探讨一下鸭子，养鸭在中国确实是一种非常有利可图的家禽养殖形式。鸭肉在这里是相当有意义的，它也是明显负担得起的健康的蛋白质。但我也在《圣经》中读到，在《路得记》里，食物短缺和饥荒影响了社会和人们的行为。

If we are to look at food and foreign policy influence, China will continue to win because an acquired taste for Chinese foods has created a global movement of this ethnic food. For discussion, we are focusing on the duck as an item of food that has been widely sent from China, through the adventurous travels of Chinese nationals, carrying with them the culture of food.

在食品和外交政策的影响方面，中国同样表现出色，因为品尝中国美食已经创造了这种民族美食的全球流动。为了便于此书中的讨论，我们将重点放在鸭肉上，随着中国国民的冒险旅行，中国的饮食文化包括食鸭文化也被从中国带到了国外。

Taking note that duck was incorporated to the delight of early Chinese emperors, it is not difficult to note that in the agenda of state relations, this intangible, but exceptional art of preparing duck as a treat with origin in China, is proudly retained.

The exchange of food gifts among heads of state and government should be noted, to the extent that almost all nations have used this custom to build friendships and create openings for discussions, thereby creating better understanding among peoples. Countries of the world have named a national dish. In the eye of this foreigner, while in China duck is a top national dish. I call for a proclamation, in recognition of this remarkable dish!

要知道中国早期皇帝们是很喜爱鸭肉的，因此这种源自中国的特殊的烹饪鸭子的艺术能被保留下来也是不难理解的。

食物和外交政策也被很好地纳入了国家关系的议程。从国家元首和政府首脑之间交换食物礼物来建立友谊，增进理解，到几乎所有的国家都有一道国宴足可证明。在我这个外国人眼里，我觉得烤鸭是一道顶级国菜。

In almost every culture food plays an important role not only for its indispensable prominence in nutrition or sustenance, but also as an identifying cultural label. A prime example in Grenadian culture, my homeland, one says oil-down, and you would be reminded that's the national dish. This is a dish cooked in coconut milk until all the milk is absorbed, leaving a bit of coconut oil in the bottom of the pot. The dish comprises a mixture of salted pigtail, pig's feet (trotters), salt beef and chicken, dumplings made from flour, with other provisions, such as breadfruit (a must) green banana, yam, potatoes, and other vegetables. Callaloo leaves cover the ingredients to retain the steam and extra flavor. Could you tell that's an all-in-one pot dish? But there is also Indian influence as seen in dhal puri, rotis, Indian sweets and curries in the Grenadian cuisine, which further explains that cuisine reveals cultural values.

几乎在大多数文化中，食物都扮演着重要的角色，这不仅仅是因为它在营养或温饱方面的不可或缺的突出地位，还因为它也是一种文化标签。举个例子，在我的家乡格林纳达，你说 "Oil-down"，我们立刻就知道，那是一道国菜。我们将咸猪尾、猪蹄（蹄膀）、咸牛肉和鸡肉混合，加入面粉团，配上面包果、绿香蕉、山药和土豆，所有这些用椰奶煮沸，直到所有的奶都被吸收，在锅底留下一点椰油就可以了。有时我们还会覆上加勒比的一种绿蔬菜叶来保留水蒸气，增加独特的味道。就是这样集多种食物在一起一锅炖便成了"Oil down"。格林纳达的菜肴也颇受印度面点，印度甜点和咖喱等的影响，这也进一步揭示了食物传递的文化价值。

The mention of Indian influence in Grenadian cookery should not surprise anyone understanding that people as they immigrate, by whatever force that moves them, hold on to their cultures. Food culture is one that is secured through the ages.

提到格林纳达饮食文化受印度饮食文化的影响，这并不足为奇，因为无论是什么样的力量促使人移民，在其移民的过程中，都会坚持自己的文化，而饮食文化无疑是一定会被流传下去的。

Food and romance must be mentioned when discussing how Chinese citizens relate to each other.   Caution is advised because there are several dishes that evoke romantic urges. Thoughts of these dishes may have you licking your fingers. It may not be culturally acceptable depending on where you are, as public romance may not be tolerated at the table.

在探讨人际关系时，食物和爱情的关系也是值得一提的，好吃的食物可能会让你忍不住舔手指，或者想要亲吻与你共同进餐的另一半，但公共场合中，这可不是被进餐礼仪所允许的。

One might conclude that duck is romance-related, because throughout the ages, certain foods have been considered aphrodisiacs. Other foods are saved for intimate moments, and, in many cases, for national, official ceremonies with high dignitaries. Some foods may be chosen because they are highly expensive and convey some measure of regard for the status of the `guest. Sometimes it is to create impressions that result in more engaging discourse.

有人或许会得出结论，说食鸭与爱情有关，因为几个世纪以来，某些食物被认为具有催情作用，会被留给亲密的时刻食用。而在许多情况下，有些食物也因贵重而多用于国家和正式礼仪中，供高级官员享用。通过这些贵重的食物一方面传达了对客人地位的一定尊重，另一方面也是为了产生更引人入胜的对话效果。

However, because Chinese food is as diverse as its cultural heritage, it would take volumes to present all. And there are volumes written about the vast creative styles of Chinese culinary arts. As the grand civilization continues to be unveiled to the world, in this new era of the twenty-first century; disclosures of many aspects of the culture have penetrated societies around the world. As the stage is set with China's leadership roles in environmental science, electronic commerce, transportation, and other developments, one realizes that cuisine has long gone ahead of other areas of development and infiltrated countless corners of the world. There is no doubt that the migration of Chinese nationals throughout the world, which began before the modern concept of globalization, Chinese carried the food preparation culture. Food is one of the largest industries of China.

然而，由于中国美食与其文化遗产一样多元，要展示出所有的内容需要大量篇幅。有大量著作探讨了中国烹饪艺术的丰富创意风格。随着中国这个伟大的文明在21世纪新时代继续向世界展现，这也揭示了许多渗透到世界各地的中国文化方面的信息。中国在环境科学、电子商务、交通等21世纪发展领域发挥领导作用的同时，人们意识到中国烹饪早已领先于其他领域的发展，并渗透到了世界各个角落。毫无疑问，中国国民在全球范围内的迁移，早在现代全球化的概念出现之前就已经开始，而他们将自己的食品制备文化带到了世界各地。食品是中国最大的产业之一。

There is so much one can learn about a people by examining the culture of food. Therefore, food as an educational tool provides insights into the values and unique aspects of people's sophistication and the complexity of the society and its inhabitants. These are duly conveyed in their way of cooking and sharing a meal.

Looking at the duck dish, and some truth about how duck (kao ya) is prepared and served in fine style and eaten as nutriment in China as a custom, is quite revealing.

通过对饮食文化的研究，可以增进对一个民族的了解。因此，食物作为一种教育工具，提供了对人们的价值观和民族先进性的深刻见解；中国社会及其居民的复杂性在他们烹饪和分享食物的方式中得到了适当的传达。

烤鸭这道菜展示出了中国人是如何以精美的风格烹调和摆盘的，这种习俗是很有启示意义的。

The information shared here is compiled from data found in public domain on the Internet, from cookbooks, personal observation, and dialogue with duck establishments. Many foreigners and Chinese citizens alike have given duck some attention. All pictures have been taken by me; mainly with my mobile phone in restaurant settings, with permission. These pictures were motivated by my appreciation of the chefs or duck carvers, and the arty carving skills demonstrated on the bird.

Did you know that the carvers are specially trained? You can be trained to bake and cut duck, but you will have to agree to be employed by the restaurant that trains you.

In addition, when one listens to the conversations taking place at mealtime, the kitchen or a restaurant table becomes a foreign policy setting for global diplomacy, which deserves close attention. This is particularly so in societies where food is part of the indigenous culture and helps to express true feelings in enjoyment and conversation at mealtime.

这里我所分享的信息来源于互联网和一些食谱，以及我个人观察及与厨师们的对话。书中所有照片都是由作者本人用其手机拍摄的。这些照片的拍摄出于对厨师们的赞赏和对他们高超技艺的敬佩。

你知道切鸭肉的师傅都是需要经过特殊培训的吗？通过同意受雇于某个烤鸭店，也可以成为烤鸭店的学徒，接受培训，学习烤鸭的烤制和切盘。

此外，在外交中，餐厅里的交流也是文化交流的一部分，尤其当今社会，食物已然成为我们文化的一部分，这些都值得我们关注。

此外，当人们聆听餐桌上的对话时，厨房或餐厅的餐桌也成为了全球外交的一个场景，值得密切关注。这在那些食物是土著文化的一部分，并且有助于在用餐时表达真实感受的社会中尤为突出。

The unified way in which a meal is provided and eaten incites the realization that food is more than nutrition. And I agree here with Johanna Mendelson Forman and Tara Sonenshine, who said in an article on March 2, 2014, that… "next to breathing, it is the most basic of human needs. mixed with culture and ethnicity, food is a powerful ingredient in human and foreign relations. It is how individuals and societies relate to one another".

食物的准备和食用的一致性让人们认识到食物带来的不仅仅是营养。在这一点上，我同意乔安娜·门德尔森·福尔曼和塔拉·索南沙因的观点，她们在2014年3月2日的一篇文章中说过："食物是仅次于呼吸的人类最基本的需求，与文化和种族相联系，食物也是人与外交关系中的一个强大因素，将个人和社会紧紧相连"。

One very interesting characteristic I have observed at the table is what I interpret as respect for each other; as demonstrated in serving each other and even when there is silence at the table. During a meal there are courtesies extended to one another that seem innate. These are most admirable displays of respect.

我在餐桌上观察到的一个非常有趣的特点，人们会互相给对方夹菜，不说话的时候也有一定的礼节，这似乎是中国人与生俱来的被视为中国人对彼此尊重的最令人钦佩的表现之一。

The relationship observed between the people of China and food enriches public diplomacy, in China and globally. This aspect of culture holds great significance, as it is well established in world history that rivals used food to negotiate and settle disputes.

American universities offer courses of studies in culinary diplomacy and conflict cuisines, in recognition of the growing importance of the food industry around the world.

我观察到的中国人和食物的关系，丰富了中国乃至全球的公共外交，中国文化在这一方面具有重大意义。在世界历史上，对手利用食物来谈判和解决争端也是众所周知的事实。在美国，各大学现在都开设了"烹饪外交"和"冲突饮食"课程，意在让人们认识到世界各地食品工业的重要性。

Instead of enduring Cold Wars among nations why not serve the disagreeable parties cold duck? As one eats, it must be remembered that food has been and is used as a weapon. Instead, let's observe the Chinese style of serving each other. Such transfer of respect can go a long way in defusing conflicts among people. I feel confident that the peacefulness of mealtime in China contributes to the harmonious nature of the society.

与其忍受国家间的冷战，不如一起吃一顿鸭子凉拌？食物曾经和现在都被当成武器一般。看看中国式的相互服务，这种尊重的传递或许可以在很大程度上化解人与人之间的冲突；我相信中国用餐时的宁静氛围为社会的和谐特性做出了贡献。

Looking at how widespread duck is served worldwide we should be reminded that citizen diplomacy can be put to work within nations by taking advantage of the Chinese diasporas to promote people to people, food diplomacy for peace and stimulate the food culture for peace and harmony. So, why not start with the well-established duck meal? Visitors to China are generally impressed by the hospitable way roast duck is prepared. It makes one feel that the hospitality displayed   could be considered a high characteristic reflected in many areas of Chinese principles, which should not go unnoticed by foreign travelers there.

看看烤鸭在全世界的普及程度，我们或许可以利用华人的优势，促进人与人之间的交流，促进和平的饮食外交，激发和谐的饮食文化，以发挥国家间公民外交的作用。那么，何不从历史悠久的食鸭开始呢？来到中国的游客一般都会被烤鸭店的好客方式留下深刻印象。烤鸭店所表现出的热情好客可以说高度体现了中国特色。

In the arena of diplomacy noted for protocols and courtesies, the art of roast duck handling and the act or process of getting it to the table are real lessons in respect and the understanding of customer service that other societies can emulate. In Chinese tradition and culture of dining, the reflection of a most peaceful and gracious acceptance of a meal when served, as a gift, with delight, and in a communally and reciprocally upright manner and sharing, with each other are remarkable.

在以礼节著称的外交领域，中国人处理烤鸭的艺术和将其送上餐桌的过程在客户服务方面所表现出来的尊重和理解，对于其他国家来说，是值得学习的一课。 中国的传统和餐饮文化中所表现出来的这种最平和，最亲切的上菜之道，将食物作为礼物， 以 一 种 共 同 互 惠 的 方 式 与 对 方 分 享 ， 这 是 非 常 了 不 起 的 。

Chapter 2
The Origin of the word duck
第2章
"鸭子"这一词的起源

Now, did you know that the origin of the word "duck" comes from the Old English *ducan* "to dive"? It is exceedingly difficult to duck the temptation of good duck portions as prepared in China. Try as you may the sight and olfactory stimulation will raise the appetite for duck. The drama in making the duck all brown and positioned on the trolley for supervised carving is an invitation to sit and stop the moving table for a taste. If you have not been to a duck restaurant in China, your imagination compels you to go and savor the dish. The environments in the restaurants that serve duck vary, yet there is that aroma of duck roasting on the open flames where the clay oven is used that makes one famished. Let your mind uncover a most enticing plate of duck, one of China's most celebrated cuisines. Now that your taste buds have begun to tingle, let us explore some more.

你知道鸭子"duck"一词起源于古英语词汇"ducan"吗？ "ducan "有"潜水"之意。在中国，鸭子的每个部分都可以被炮制出各式各样的美食，所以要抵制住这种诱惑，是极为困难的。你尽管试，来自视觉和嗅觉的感官冲击，会让你的食欲飙升。上桌前，师傅们推着烤成褐色的鸭子准备精心切片，就像是给你发出邀请，让你坐下来开始品尝。如果你还没有去过中国的烤鸭店，你的想象力也会迫使你去品尝这道菜。提供烤鸭的餐厅环境各不相同，但在使用土炉的明火上烤鸭的香味总是让人饥肠辘辘。所以，去发现那一盘最诱人的烤鸭吧，这可是中国最著名的美食之一。我相信现在你的味蕾已经开始兴奋了，我们下面更加深入的探讨一下这道美食的前世今生。

But what is a duck?
何为鸭？

Duck is a water bird. Duck is the female, and the male is called drake. Numerous species are included within this bird family; there are the domesticated ducks, which descended from wild mallard ducks. Ducks are found in many regions of the world, in both salt and freshwater environments, and they are a common feature of barnyards, thanks to their gentle dispositions.

众所周知，鸭子是一种水禽。但你知道雌性的鸭子我们叫"duck"，而雄性的被称为"drake"吗？ 鸭子家族包括众多的物种，有驯化的鸭子，它们是野鸭的后代。鸭子在世界许多地区，无论是咸水还是淡水环境中都能找到，畜牧场也常见，这要归功于它们温和的习性。

In addition to duck's flavorful flesh, let us take a quick look at nutritional values of duck eggs vs chicken eggs: Research shows that: "Duck's egg has six times the Vitamin D, twice the Vitamin A, and two times the cholesterol in duck eggs compared to chicken eggs. Duck contains about 75% of the Vitamin E in chicken eggs." Duck eggs researchers say that duck eggs also have more Vitamin K2. Duck eggs are higher in calories for the same weight quantity, probably due to its slightly higher fat concentration. However, it must be remembered that the eggs of free-range, animals raised on pasture generally have higher levels of vitamins and higher levels of omega-3 fatty acids. The yolks are darker, yellower, indicating a higher nutrient density.

除了鸭子的肉质鲜美之外，鸭蛋也是美味。让我们快速了解一下鸭蛋与鸡蛋的营养价值：研究表明，鸭蛋中的维生素 D 是鸡蛋的六倍，维生素 A 是鸡蛋的两倍，胆固醇是鸡蛋的两倍。鸭子的维生素E含量约为鸡蛋的75%。研究人员说鸭蛋还有更多的维生素K2，鸭蛋在相同重量下热量也更高，可能是由于其脂肪浓度略高。在农场饲养的动物的鸡蛋通常含更高的维生素和更高的欧米茄-3 脂肪酸。蛋黄颜色更深，更黄，表明营养程度更高。

Duck eggs compared to chicken eggs.

Duck eggs are an alkaline producing food - anti cancer food – and are considered much better than chicken eggs. But whether it is farm fresh eggs, with a rich smooth orange yolk, chicken eggs or duck eggs will surprise you, if you have only experienced the colorless and flavorless supermarket versions. Many people seem not to know that duck eggs are far superior to chicken eggs, with the same taste but a richer, smoother consistency making the duck eggs better than a chicken egg in many ways.

鸭蛋与鸡蛋的比较。

鸭蛋是一种可以产生碱的食物，具有抗癌作用，被认为比鸡蛋好得多。如果你只吃过超市里售卖的无色无味的鸡蛋或者鸭蛋，当你试过农场鲜蛋，配上浓郁光滑的橙色蛋黄，无论是鸡蛋还是鸭蛋口感都会让你感到吃惊。大多数人可能都不知道，鸭蛋远远优于鸡蛋，虽然具有相似的味道，但营养更丰富，在许多方面都比鸡蛋更好。

1. Duck eggs have twice the nutritional value of chicken eggs and stay fresher longer due to their thicker shell.
2. Duck eggs are richer with more Albumen, making cakes and pastries fluffier and

3. Duck eggs have more Omega 3 fatty acids; something you can see in the salted pickled eggs the Chinese love to eat. Omega 3 is thought to improve everything from brain health to healthy skin.

4. Duck eggs are an alkaline producing food, one of the few foods that leave your body more alkaline, which is a great benefit to cancer patients as cancer cells do not thrive in an alkaline environment. Chicken eggs are an acid food, leaving your body more acidic. There is one reason why many people are hesitant to try a duck egg and that is that the yolk contains about a one-day supply of Cholesterol. This is not good for heart diseases. This depends on what you believe about weight control and fat or cholesterol. *Taken from posting on Bing Search Engine, by Evergreen Acres Goat Farm (Tres Pinos, California)*
。

1. 鸭蛋的营养价值是鸡蛋的两倍，而且由于鸭蛋的蛋壳更厚，所以能保鲜更长时间。

2. 鸭蛋含有更多的白蛋白，使蛋糕和糕点更松软。

3. 鸭蛋有更多的欧米茄 3 脂肪酸。从中国人喜欢吃咸鸭蛋这一点就可以看出来。欧米茄 3 脂肪酸被认为可以使大脑更健康，皮肤更光泽。

4. 鸭蛋是为数不多的使你身体呈碱性的食物之一，这对癌症患者有很大的好处，因为癌细胞在碱性环境中无法生长。鸡蛋是一种酸性食物，使你的身体更偏向于酸性。许多人不敢尝试鸭蛋的一个原因是蛋黄含有大约你 1 天的可摄入的胆固醇供应量。这对心脏病患者不利。这取决于你对体重控制和脂肪或胆固醇的看法。（摘自必应搜索引擎上的 帖子，由加利福尼亚州特雷斯皮诺斯一处农场提供）

Look at the unique color of duck eggs
鸭蛋呈现出与众不同的表皮颜色

(joke) (The difference between a duck is both legs just the same) Several features distinguish ducks from other water birds. Ducks have muscular bodies built for diving and dredging, with short legs and webbed feet that allow them to navigate a watery environment. Ducks also have distinctive broad, flat bills to root through water grasses and mud, as well as snap up various preys and plant materials.

（笑话）（鸭子的区别在于它们两只腿都一样）鸭子与其他水禽有几个明显的区别。鸭子有健壮的肌肉所以可以拨开污泥潜入水下，还有短腿和蹼可以在水域游行，他们还有与众不同的扁平的嘴，因而可以穿过水草和污泥，捕捉到猎物和植物饲料。

On the water, ducks look quite graceful, as their bodies are adapted to swimming. On land, however, ducks look rather awkward and wobbly, because their legs are set far back on their bodies, causing them to have a waddling gait. Ducks are capable of flight, except when they are shedding, and some duck species make long annual migration journey to mate and raise young.

在水中，鸭子通常看起来非常优美，因为它们的身体适应了游泳。然而，在陆地上，鸭子看起来相当笨拙和摇摇摆摆，因为它们的腿位于身体的后部，导致它们有摇摆的步态。如果不是脱羽，鸭子也具备飞行的能力。还有一些品种的鸭子每年都会进行长途迁徙以交配和繁殖幼崽。

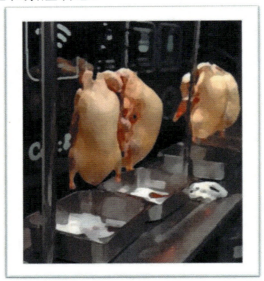

<u>Featherless fresh duck traditionally hung, before baking</u>
烤制前，脱毛的新鲜的鸭子通常被挂起来

We know what the male and female ducks are called; do you know what baby ducks are known as? "ducklings" Generally, it takes around a year for a duck to fully mature. You could now imagine that mature ducks are not the only ducks at your table. Ducks and drakes pair off briefly during mating season to mate and raise their ducklings. Most duck species are sexually dimorphic, with brightly colored males and more drab females. Sexual dimorphism means that there are differences in appearance between males and females of the same species, such as color, shape, size, and structure. These qualities are caused by the heritage of one or the other sexual pattern in the genetic make- up.

我们知道了公鸭子和母鸭子的名字区别。您知道小鸭子叫"duckling"吗？鸭子一般需要一年左右才能完全成熟。所以你可以想象，成熟的鸭子并不是您餐桌上唯一的鸭子。公鸭和母鸭在交配季节交配，产出小鸭。大多数鸭子都是两性异形的，毛色鲜艳的为公，颜色相对单调的为母。两性异形意味着同一物种的雄性和雌性在外观上存在差异，如颜色，身形，大小和结构。这些特点是由基因组成中遗传模式引起的。

The male duck comes in a wide range of sizes and colored feathers, with some drakes having decorative crests and other interesting physical features, which make them stand out from a flock. Among domesticated ducks, in addition to the common white Peking duck, there is a wide variety of duck. These include the Blue Cayuga, the Crested Swedish, Khaki Campbell, Mallard, Indian Runner, and the charmingly ugly Muscovy duck, which has a bald neck and head. There are farmed ducks, domesticated ducks and wild ducks, which are divided into several groups, including perching, diving and dabbling ducks.

公鸭叫"drake"，通常体型大小不一，羽毛鲜艳，还有些鸭子有着装饰似的冠和其它有趣的身体特征，从而让他们有"鹤立鸭群"的感觉。家养的鸭子中，除了常见的白色北京鸭外，还有各种各样的鸭子：有蓝色的卡尤加鸭、有凤头瑞典鸭、卡其·坎贝尔鸭、绿头鸭、印度跑鸭，还有又丑又可爱的疣鼻栖鸭，秃脖子秃头。还有养殖鸭、家鸭和野鸭，它们被分成若干组：栖鸭、潜鸭和钻水鸭。

Quacking is generally associated with ducks; however, not many duck's species quack. Instead, ducks make a range of other calls, which are used to communicate with other ducks in a flock. Contrary to traditional local stories that a duck's quack does not echo, a duck's quack will, in fact echo. One must just listen.

嘎嘎叫一般被认为是鸭子的特征，然而能嘎嘎叫的鸭子种类并不多。相反，鸭子有各种各样其他的叫声，用来和鸭群里其他鸭子交流。民间有种说法，"鸭子的叫声没有回声"，但只要你仔细听就知道事实并非如此。

Ducks may be some of the most familiar bird species even to non- birdwatchers; but what makes a duck, a duck? The unique characteristics of these waterfowl are often overlooked and underappreciated in their diversity, but people who understand how to define ducks can better enjoy these feathered wonders: beyond dining, even for the show and use of their luxurious feathers. Duck is one of more than10, 000 unique species of birds in the world.

对于不观鸟的人来说，鸭子可能是他们最熟悉的鸟类之一了。鸭子的本质到底是什么？因为品种繁多，它们独有的特征经常被人忽视，但是真正懂得如何定义鸭子的人更能赏识它们的奇妙。除去食用外，鸭子还可以用于观赏，羽毛也十分漂亮。鸭子是世界上一万多种独特的鸟类之中的一种。

The discussion about the individualities of the duck and all the fine qualities, along with the uniqueness of this type of feathered friend, prompts the thought about the inimitable characteristics transmitted by citizens of the People's Republic of China.

The attributes of the people are most visible on openings that provide for their demonstration of mutual pride and respect for country, patriotism and embrace of the culture.

关于鸭子个性的讨论，以及这种有羽毛的朋友所有优良品质和独特性，都使我们想起中国人传递的不可模仿的特性。中国人民的品质似乎在公开场合最为明显，尤其表现为相互尊重，热爱祖国和高度拥护其文化的自豪感。

China's success in feeding its population has been cited for the valuable lessons provided to developing countries worldwide. The lessons shared further unveil characteristics, as shown by the way leaders and policymakers across China have embraced initiatives such as Healthy China 2030 initiative. Such focus on the welfare of people provides a good model for the developing world.

中国在养活其人口方面的成功为全世界的发展中国家提供了宝贵的经验。中国分享的经验进一步揭示了中国人善于计划的特点，中国各地的领导和政策制定者接受"健康中国 2030"等倡议的方式就表明了这一点。这种对人民福利的关注为其他发展中国家提供了良好的借鉴模式。

Partly because of worries about an impending food crisis, China started its reform drive by breaking up farming collectives and empowering small-scale farmers. By linking effort to reward, productivity and output sharply increased. This laid the groundwork for change throughout the economy.

部分原因是由于对即将到来的粮食危机的担忧，中国开始了其改革运动，从小农户和农村地区开始，打破了农业集体，赋予小规模农民权力，通过将努力与回报联系起来，生产力和产出急剧增加，这也为整个经济的变革奠定了基础。

China's leaders did not simply unleash agricultural markets, as Western development agencies often recommend developing countries should do. Instead, they concentrated state policies on ensuring that peasant farmers had the resources, knowledge, and necessary incentives to maximize output. The state remained firmly in control of prices (increasing them to encourage extra effort), the distribution system and the supply of fertilizer. Over time, improvements to extension services, better infrastructure, investments in agricultural research and large-scale education and training programs paid huge dividends.[5] Only after the agricultural sector strengthened, did officials introduce more widespread market liberalization reforms in the 1990s and 2000s.

但是，中国的领导人并没有像西方发展机构经常建议发展中国家做的那样，简单地开放农业市场。相反，他们把国家政策集中在确保农民拥有必要的资源、知识和激励措施，以实现产出最大化。国家仍然牢牢控制着价格（提高价格以鼓励额外的付出）、分配系统和肥料供应。随着时间的推移，推广服务的改进、基础设施的完善、对农业研究的投资以及大规模的教育和培训项目，给人民带来了巨大的红利。直到农业部门得到加强后，中国官员才在 1990 年代和 2000 年代引入了更广泛的市场自由化改革政策。

Today, many of China's most successful private manufacturing firms are based in or got their start in relatively underdeveloped, predominantly agricultural areas. The New Hope Group, one of China's largest private businesses, started as a breeding farm raising quail and poultry in rural Sichuan. Kelon, one of China's largest white goods manufacturers, was founded in rural Shunde county in southern Guandong. China's most promising automobile exporter, Chery, is based not in Shanghai, but in the agricultural hinterland of Anhui province. Success in the food industry can be attributed to the people's growing confidence in their leaders and that seems to make the leaders feel more accountable to their people. Even in the way they eat and what they eat demonstrates strong national identity. The culture promotes sociology as being more important than economics. Keeping the people satisfied and happy is a key element in the strength of the common cultural identity and group allegiance that exist in China.

如今，中国许多最成功的私营制造企业都位于或起步于相对不发达、以农业为主的地区。新希望集团是中国最大的私营企业之一，起初是在四川农村经营鹌鹑和家禽养殖场。科龙是中国最大的家电制造商之一，成立于广东南部顺德县的农村地区。而中国最有前途的汽车出口商，奇瑞，总部位于安徽省农村腹地，而不是上海。食品行业的成功可以归因于人们对领导者的信任日益增强，这似乎使领导者对待他们的人民更有责任感。甚至他们吃饭的方式和食物都展示了强烈的民族认同。中国有一种文化倡导将社会学视为比经济学更重要的领域。让人民满意和幸福是中国共同文化认同和群体忠诚力量的关键因素。

As earlier mentioned, it is worth repeating that there is a dominant history and cultural consciousness that remain on the surface of all engagement of the people. As research has disclosed pragmatism and flexibility are noticeable traits.

如前所述，值得重申的是，有一种占主导地位的历史和文化意识，它在人们的所有交往中都有体现，那就是实用主义和灵活性。

Chapter 3
Chinese etiquette while dining

第三章
中国就餐礼节

If you are still wondering, why the focus is on duck; it is proven that ducks are not like other birds; and the quality of the protein in duck meat is different from other proteins.

In the case of duck meat, being different does not mean deficient; it is assessed to be better. Duck meat protein is a delicious, nutritious alternative to other poultry or beef that stands up to any seasoning and maintains its flavor and taste. All its features stand out.

现在我们都知道，鸭子与其他鸟类不同，鸭肉中蛋白质的品质也和其他蛋白质不同。鸭肉的"不同"并不意味着不好，反而是更好。鸭肉的蛋白质是牛肉、鸡肉等的完美替代品，可以随意调味，其味道和特征也独树一帜。

The taste of duck is more than delicious. The question that pops up is, what does duck taste like? It depends on whose duck one tastes. That certainly also has to do with its preparation. Peking duck has a red meat flavor, that's more like beef steak than of chicken or turkey, and it's a nutritious substitute, equally suited for a main course meal. However, the preparation must be mentioned as a most significant aspect of its appeal. The good news about duck is that when it is properly cooked, 70% of the fat can be drained. Duck is leaner and has less saturated fat than other meats. Still, it is quite admirable to see the care taken by the servers, not only to prepare the meal but to present and lay out the dish with respect in a dutiful manner that reflects courtesy, honor in serving and pleasing the diners as family members rather than patrons.

鸭肉的味道不是"美味"二字所能描述的。鸭肉尝起来什么样？这要取决于您吃的是哪种鸭。北京烤鸭有一种牛羊肉的味道，比起鸡肉或火鸡，尝起来和牛排更相近，而且可以作为鸡肉和火鸡的营养替代品。鸭肉的优点就是，鸭子做熟以后70%的脂肪都会流失，从而使鸭肉比其他肉类更瘦，饱和脂肪更少。当你看到大厨们不仅精心备菜，而且以独特的方式上菜，这场景令人肃然起敬，吃的人会感觉自己不是普通的食客而是有被当作家人一样对待。

Duck seems easy to prepare for everyday meals and is perfect for special occasions. The dish can be incorporated into a wide range of flavor profiles and cuisines to create culinary adventurers everywhere.

鸭子很容易烹制，适合平时吃也适合特殊场合享用。鸭肉可以被融入进多种口味的菜肴和菜系中，可以创造出各种各样的新菜品。

Did you know of the claim made, that duck fat has similar health benefits to olive oil and other unsaturated fats? Duck fits well into healthy lifestyles, so one can enjoy the rich flavor of duck's meat without guilt of the bulge.

你知道有人说鸭肉的脂肪和橄榄油等其他不饱和脂肪有着相似的健康效果吗？鸭肉非常适合现代健康的生活方式，所以人们可以毫无罪恶感地享受美味的鸭肉，吃完也不会长胖。

A review of the nutritional facts of duck or drake meat may well entice eating more duck, after looking at the comparison with duck's feathered friend chicken other birds and even pork.

对鸭肉的营养研究，为吃货们提供了非常有趣的营养事实，在与鸭子的羽毛朋友鸡、其他鸟类甚至猪进行比较后，人们可能会更倾向于吃鸭肉。

Delicate separation of duck parts at a restaurant in Beijing
Watching how the duck is carved presents an interesting artistic performance

鸭肉的切片过程是一场非常有趣的艺术表演

Now that so much has been learned about duck, all questions can be answered about duck. So, what is the difference between a duck? Have you found the Answer on page 20? No. That was an attempted joke at mealtime.

现在对鸭子已经了解了很多，关于鸭子的所有问题都可以得到回答。那么，鸭子之间有什么区别呢？你在第20页找到答案了吗？并没有。这只是在用餐时试图开个玩笑而已。

There is an enlightening, informative and amusing elucidation, which contributes to one's admiration for the manner by which persons of Chinese heritage display respect for each other. In addition, unbiased observation unearths the high value of a welcoming meal for the advancement of cordial relations in public diplomacy and bilateral relations as an effective tool to strengthen people to people and diplomatic relations.

这里提供了一个富有启发性、信息丰富和有趣的阐述，这些内容增加了人们对中国文化传承者在用餐习俗中彼此表现出互相尊重方式的欣赏。此外，你也可以观察发现，欢迎的餐食对于促进公共外交和双边关系的和睦关系尤为重要，可作为加强人际和外交关系的有效工具。

The poise, pleasure, pomp, and respectful engaging ways Chinese exhibit as they dine are refreshing. The significance of the rituals in preparing the duck dish is observed as being grateful. The cultural values commemorated are done with pageantry, drama and pride in the way chefs display roasting duck. Roast duck/Piking duck is among China's

n

the rich respect and harmony of Chinese people toward each other. But why duck, where did the tradition of this majestic and stately preparation of this popular food begin? These questions have many angles.

中国人在就餐时表现出的风度、愉悦、隆重和尊重他人的态度，令人耳目一新。在准备烤鸭的过程中，人们看到了仪式的意义，它表达了一种感恩之情。厨师们在制作烤鸭的过程中所表现出来的仪式和自豪感也是文化价值的体现。烤鸭是中国著名的美食，也是中国最受欢迎的美食之一。享用这一美食的时刻也彰显了中国人对彼此的尊重和中国人民的和谐相处之道。那你知道准备这种美食的仪式传统是从什么时候开始兴起的吗？这个答案有多种说法。

The world knows that beside the duck at the revolving table, is a good bowl of "Yangzhou's Fried Rice" which seems to be able to open hearts and minds, not just to the peaceful dining on mainland and other parts of the Chinese world, but for its promotion of peaceful coexistence among Chinese people. Yangzhou's Fried Rice was passed to Yangzhou, by Emperor Yang of Sui Dynasty. Well-made Yangzhou fried rice is said to look like glittering broken gold and tastes delicious.

现在全世界都知道，在旋转餐桌上，烤鸭旁边，会有一碗上好的"扬州炒饭"，它似乎能够打开人们的心扉，它的重要性不仅仅体现在它可以让华人在世界的各个地方和平用餐，也可以促进中国人民的和平共处。扬州炒饭是由隋炀帝传到扬州的。据说，制作精良的扬州炒饭看起来像闪闪发光的碎金，吃起来也很美味。

It is fitting that the China Public Diplomacy Association sees it fit to promote this Silk Road City Cuisine in Yangzhou; a city known for traditional gardens and alleys,' and as a retainer of ancient Chinese architecture, art, culture, parks, cuisine, and commerce. The cultural heritage, as reflected in duck dining and Yangzhou fried rice, is believed to have a beautiful mixture of modernity, with a rich 2500-years of socio-cultural history.

中国公共外交协会认为在扬州推广丝绸之路城市美食是非常合适的，扬州是一个以传统花园和小巷闻名的城市，保留着中国古代的建筑、艺术、文化、公园、美食和商业。中国的文化遗产很好地反映在鸭肉菜肴和扬州炒饭中，被认为是现代性与具有2500年悠久中国社会文化历史的美丽结合。

It is understood that culinary diplomacy is all about connecting individuals, leaders, and nations through food. In many countries food festivals are organized to promote cuisine by bringing chefs to work in embassies for the promotion of national dishes. There is something uniquely special about food. Family friends and people, everywhere, always come together around food.

众所周知，烹饪外交就是通过食物将个人、领导人和国家联系起来。许多国家都举办美食节，通过邀请厨师到大使馆工作，来推广本国美食。食物有其独特之处，不管在哪里，家人朋友们总是喜欢围着食物而坐。

It is worth repeating that "The destiny of nations depends on how they nourish themselves." As peoples move, they carry their foods with them, and the memory of the foods they crave. When cultures come in contact where meals are prepared in the kitchens, at the family dining tables, official banquets, picnics and restaurants, a peaceful scene unfolds. Cultural diplomacy also occurs when people promote the sharing of values, traditions, and worldviews, worldwide, through food.

值得重复强调的是"国家的命运取决于它们如何滋养自己"。随着人们的迁徙，他们将自己的食物和对美食的记忆带到新的地方。当不同文化相遇时，无论是在家庭餐桌上、官方宴会上、野餐和餐馆中，一幕幕平和的场景展现。文化外交也随之产生，因为人们通过食物在全世界范围内分享交流不同的价值观、传统和世界观。

The influence of the culinary traditions, as unveiled with Yangzhou rice, is indeed a most welcoming way of sharing the customs, culture and hospitable traditions of China. That's why duck is elevated to a national heritage secret of China, and is worth exploration for its global reach and impact on the palate of the world's peoples. Eating Peking Duck/roast duck, with crispy skin and moist, flavorful flesh in Taipei, with spring onions and plum sauce in small pancakes, is an exclamation of the feeling that duck is regarded as being a unifying force and a high point of Chinese cuisine.

烹饪传统的影响，正如扬州炒饭所揭示的那样，是分享中国的习俗、文化和好客传统的一种最受欢迎的方式。这就是为什么烤鸭被提升为中国国家遗产的秘密，值得人们探索其对世界人民饮食口味产生的影响。在台北吃北京烤鸭，皮酥肉润，味道鲜美，配上葱和梅子酱，放在小煎饼里，让人深深觉得烤鸭是一种统一的力量，也是中国美食的亮点之一。

Chapter 4
Medicinal functions of duck, according to traditional Chinese medicine (TCM)

第4章
鸭肉的药用疗效，中医之说

According to traditional Chinese medicine, duck is a cold-natured food. It is an excellent tonic food that nourishes the stomach and is used for toning kidneys, treating edemas, relieving coughs, and reducing phlegm. One could agree that the long history of this nutritional intake provides ample longitudinal evidence of this claim by traditional Chinese medicine (TCM). It is widely established that duck is a popular meat in the main course as the table turns at mealtimes and is served with pride and Chinese cordiality.

中医认为，鸭肉性凉，和胃消食，常用于治疗肾虚水肿、止咳化痰。中国人吃鸭肉的悠久历史为传统中医的这一说法提供了充分的证据。人们普遍认为，鸭肉是主菜中最受欢迎的肉类，不仅仅因为烤鸭餐桌的转动，还因为服务人员亲切诚挚的上菜方式 。

There are so many variations of delightful presentations with admiration of the honorable modes in which duck is rolled out in the various provinces of China. Strangely the bird is not often seen before it comes to the table; however, there is fanfare in the way it is carved and presented right before your eyes. It seems like nowhere else in the world is such ceremony observed with drama and satisfaction in bringing the duck dish to the menu, ready for the meal event. Wielding the razor-sharp knife the chef looking waiter cuts into the succulent skin of the greased roasted duck, then the breast, then carves the lean brown meat from the skeleton. With white gloves he twists and separates the short legs and wings. and lays them in a tempting presentation to the dining customers' delight.

用鸭肉制成的菜肴花样丰富，深得人们喜爱。上桌之前的鸭子人们通常看不到，但其切割摆盘方式却很有讲究。世界上任何其他地方都不曾有这样的仪式，过程极其盛大、富有戏剧性，大厨如雕刻雕像一般用锋利的刀先切开多汁的鸭皮和鸭胸，然后切下骨头旁棕色的瘦肉，他戴着白色手套，把鸭腿和鸭翅扭下，摆在盘中，诱惑着食客。

Duck's ratings as one of China's best-known dishes is maintained among the most popular dining establishments. The varied styles of duck seem endless ass if traditional Chinese medicine's claim to duck being wholesome has blessed that food. This cold natured food seems to warm up one's appetite. Duck soup is believed to have the function of dispelling summer heat according to Chinese tradition.

烤鸭被认为是中国最有名的菜肴之一，是中国饮食文化中最受欢迎的传统。鸭的烹制方法好似无穷无尽。而中医也认为鸭肉很健康——鸭肉虽性凉，却能激起食欲。鸭肉能和胃消食，常用于治疗肾虚水肿、止咳化痰。鸭汤也被认为有祛暑热的功效。

Duck soup 鸭汤

It is useful to peruse the menus when the decision is made to explore dining on duck. There is formal duck dining and there are many opportunities to taste duck in informal settings. Duck meat, on the street in malls, food courts and in other fast-food venues; but it is in the informal settings that the full dimension of duck meat is revealed. The following can help one to go on a taste adventure and test one's ability to name some other parts of duck, which are prepared and served with delight, but not usually in formal settings.

当你决定在中国探索鸭肉的菜品时，要多研究菜单。在中国有许多机会在非正式场合品尝鸭肉，在街上的商场、美食广场和其他快餐场所都有鸭肉可售。在非正式场合，你才有机会看到鸭肉的全貌得以展现。你可以做下面的一个小测验，试试自己可以说出哪些鸭子的不同部位可做成的美食，这些美食一般不在正式场合出现。

Here is a menu from which to choose:以下菜单供您参考

Baked duck
Roasted duck
Boiled duck
Grilled or microwaved duck
Duck soup
Fried duck bones
Duck breast
Duck neck
焗鸭
烤鸭
炖鸭
鸭汤
鸭骨
鸭胸
鸭脖

This is a picture of duck intestines, Beijing special snack (the good old taste) on Wangfujing Snack Street

王府井小吃街的鸭肠

In China all parts of duck are made to taste good so that even duck intestines can be presented as a delicacy. Beijing specialty snacks are old and fascinating. This picture was taken in Beijing 2017.

(在中国，鸭子的每一个部分，甚至鸭肠都可以被制作成美味。)

The Street food industry in China is diverse, creative, and attractive. Better yet, appealing! The side roads are decorated with a colorful pageant of artistic displays, making foods convenient in fast moving, very crowded spaces and to look mouthwatering. In the cities and places of public interest, especially subway exits and entrances, parks, huge street corners, temples, and bus stations. It is rather fascinating for the passerby not to gaze on some of the most eye-catching food shows with indescribable selections on the menu for dining on the street dishes. Eating on the run, eating for fun and eating on the street corners, are adventures. It is an undertaking that requires nerve, a strong stomach, and a special Chinese quality courage to try. Something I observe is that Chinese have zest, and they seem to enjoy exciting activities, and when reviewing Chinese cuisine that seems to excite. Yet the vendors are so pressured to meet the demand of the large volume of customers, that one can observe some short cuts in food preparation.

中国的街头食品业多种多样，富有创意，也很吸引人。街道两旁装饰着五光十色的艺术展示，使食物在快节奏、人来人往的空间中变得方便，看起来令人垂涎。在城市和公共场所，尤其是地铁出入口、公园、街角、寺庙和汽车站等地，路人不禁会被一些最引人注目的美食展示吸引，菜单上的选择多不胜数，让人可以在街头品尝各种美味的菜肴。在奔波中就餐，享受美食，以及在街角就餐，都是一次冒险。这需要勇气和坚强的胃，以及一种特殊的中国品质，即勇敢尝试。我观察到中国人很有激情，他们似乎很喜欢刺激的活动，而在回顾中国美食时，这似乎也激发了他们的热情。然而，摊贩们在满足大量顾客需求的压力下，有时会采用一些简便的食品制备方法。

Imagine the economic reality of the food industry in China and the need to design food hubs. This truth positions Beijing at the center of one of the largest clusters of all human beings anywhere in the world. It is fascinating to think about the requirements and the logistics required for ensuring adherence to sound policy for catering and other food services necessary to feed the masses that pass-through centers like the Beijing Dashing Airport, which is a colossal, contained space at that mega airport. In addition to feeding the new tri-state, with an excess of one 130 million people, food on demand for travelers, offices, residents, and leisure is a mind-blowing undertaking. I always remember visiting and walking along Wangfujing Snack Street, which I call a street food hub in Beijing.

现在想象一下中国的食品产业面临的经济现实，以及需要设计食品中心的需求。在北京这个世界上人口最多的地区之一，想象一下要确保遵守合理的餐饮政策和其他食品服务政策所需的要求和物流设施，以满足人员流动中心的大众需求，比如北京大兴机场，这是一个巨大的封闭空间。此外，还要为旅行者、办公室员工、居民和休闲者提供点餐服务，这是一个令人惊叹的工程。我永远记得漫步在北京王府井小吃街的情景，我觉得王府井是北京的一个街头美食中心。

Wangfujing Street always seems busy, the food displays are everywhere, there are alluring snacks and fast meals that hang and dangle in the windows. At every step there is a hospitable attendant, at the booths or the windows, smiling and ready to serve with efficiency. And the smells of delicious looking, and intriguing offerings of fried insects as food, and at every corner, in every hole-in-the-wall, another food adventure. Foreigners visiting Beijing are encouraged to create some food memories, as I have done on that street. Keep an open mind and be ready to surrender to a taste of duck parts on a stick, or some other authentic offering.

王府井大街上似乎总是很热闹，到处都有食物展示，那些诱人的小吃在窗口悬空而立。你每走一步都会有一个好客的服务员，在摊位或窗口微笑着准备提供高效的服务。每一个角落里，都有看起来很美味的油炸昆虫小吃，似乎在每一个墙洞里，都散发着一种食物探险的味道。我希望来北京旅游的外国人可以像我一样，在那条街上留下一些美好的回忆。记住要保持开放的心态，品尝一下鸭肉串，或其他一些地道的小吃。

Duck can be prepared to appeal to the taste buds, to please every customer, as many as there are in China and more. I Peking duck is hailed as one of China's most famous dishes. It is not intended to focus on who does what, the focus is on what they do with the duck. With that said, Nanjing duck, the salted duck, must be hailed, simply because citizens and foreigners alike speak so "mouth- wateringly" about this dish.

烤鸭可以经过精心准备，以迎合人们的味蕾，让每位顾客都满意。众所周知，北京烤鸭被誉为中国最著名的菜肴之一。重点不在于谁制作了什么，而在于他们如何制作。因此，南京盐水鸭也应该受到称赞，因为中外人民都对这道菜赞不绝口。

The author listening for the secret of carving duck

作者在聆听烤鸭切片的秘密

Because there are so many ways to prime that bird, one needs to know how they like theirs done. Where did this tradition of majestic, stately, and appetizing plates of this bird meat begin? For most foreigners, especially when dining as a diplomat, it's easy to recall the first encounter of duck at a restaurant in China such as a meal with "Peking Duck." One wonders if there is a secret to creating the taste.

因为实在有太多方法可以烹饪鸭肉了，所以你需要知道你喜欢什么样的味道。那这种庄重，令人胃口大开的鸭肉饮食传统从何而来呢？大多数外国人，特别是外交官，吃鸭肉的经历大概都是开始于第一次在中国餐厅吃北京烤鸭。

Many pay close attention to the brown skin, baked ducks hanging by their necks in the show windows of the roadside (kao ya dian -The old traditional roast duck shops) when travelling in China or visiting 'China Towns' in the Chinese diaspora, globally. The brown, shiny, oily looking ducks look inviting.

在中国以及全球的中国城里，许多人都会注意到那些挂在烤鸭店窗口棕色闪着油光看起来很诱人的烤鸭。

The brown, shiny, oily looking ducks
色泽成棕色，油光发亮的烤鸭

Served cold sliced or whole, this master food retains intergenerational prominence in Chinese homes and communities.

这道美食以切片或整只的方式被端上餐桌，一直在中国家庭和社区中代代传承，保持着重要地位。

Get duck to take away, get duck any style; get your mode of duck. Taking cured packaged gourmet duck home for the holiday is a common gift for the family back home when visiting during the spring festival holidays. When the city dwellers take the long train ride home, they bring duck. The cost of duck seems very reasonable in China, and readily available.

你也可以买鸭肉带走，任何口味，供你选择。将包装好的美味鸭肉带回家，是春节期间中国人给家人最常见的礼物。在城里居住的人坐长途火车回家时，会带上袋装烤鸭。烤鸭的价格在中国算是比较合理的。

Chapter 5
Some history about dining in and out of China

第5章
中国内外的饮食历史

Chinese cuisine has history outside China. The preparation of duck Chinese style in the Caribbean cannot go unnoticed. There are some dishes from Chinese homes in the Caribbean that I remember and the question I am always asked. What is your favorite duck dish? Fried Duck Tongue with spicy sauce still lingers with mouthwatering impact as an adventure in eating. Be assured that it is one of the best dimensions of duck tasting.

This escapade in tasting gives another insight into the disposition of a people that has endured such a continuous legacy of feasting. When eating duck, can you tell the difference between Beijing duck and Peking duck? It depends on who answers. A Chinese citizen or a foreigner. However, differences are being identified. Just remember you can have both styles as you wish. The difference may be revealed in presentation or preparation styles, and it could depend on what generation one represents, the claim can reveal attitudes that express qualities which add up to identifying being Chinese.

中国菜在中国以外的地方也有着悠久的历史，尤其是在加勒比地区以中国风格制作的鸭肴也不容忽视。现在，很多人都知道鸭肉的多种食用方法，这让我回想起了加勒比地区的一些中国家庭美食，还有一个问题一直在我的脑海中回响：你最喜欢哪道鸭肴？我当时想到的是辣酱炒鸭舌，令人垂涎欲滴，简直像冒险一般的尝试，但可以放心，这是品尝鸭子的最佳方法之一。这种冒险让我对中国这样一个饮食文化悠久的民族性情有了另一种了解。当你吃烤鸭时，是否可以区分现在的 Beijing 烤鸭和以前的Peking烤鸭呢？嗯，这取决于问这个问题的人是中国人还是外国人，其实，两种风格尽可随心所欲。区别可能在于烹制方式或摆盘方式。这也取决于不同年代的人的不同呈现，但都可以揭示出其想要表达菜肴品质的态度。

Fatty duck skin with sugar and salt seems to be a prelude or an appetizer before the main course of duck; then comes the rich duck soup, like a tradition just as the table begins to turn. Therefore, it is then safe to call duck a capital Dish.

脆脆的鸭皮，配上糖和盐，好像是在上鸭肉主菜之前的前奏或开胃菜。接下来，餐桌转动，就会有美味的鸭汤奉上。因此，可以毫不夸张地将鸭肴称为一道"特色菜"。

But why duck? A simple deduction can be made; duck is a Chinese experience of the fifth dimension. Dining at a food establishment in China is conducive to the conduct of diplomatic meetings and productive discussions. Many ambassadors and diplomats can be found eating at duck establishments on any given day; these settings include some of the best duck menus and favorable venues for business luncheons, and meetings. Foreigners in China are excellent validators of the duck dining fascination.

但为什么大家爱吃鸭肉呢？可以做一个简单的推断；鸭肉或许是中国人饮食的第五维体验。在中国的餐饮场所用餐似乎总是有利于进行外交会议和一些富有成效的讨论。很多时候都可以看见大使和外交官在中国最好的烤鸭店或是商务午餐，或是简单会议。在中国的外国人喜欢烤鸭的程度也是烤鸭魅力的证明。

There is a kind of romance with duck dishes. Regardless of how many times one has eaten duck intestines, and you knew it was the belly of the duck, there is a denial. You keep on asking "what part of the duck is this? May I have some more because it tastes so good?" There are many ways in which duck parts are served, and you may never know that it is the same parts being served. For example, here are some of the many ways: duck intestines with chili sauce, fried duck intestines, duck intestines with green pepper, stir-fried duck Intestines with green pepper, and many options to explore.

不管你吃过多少次鸭肠，即便你知道那是鸭子的肠子，你还是会忍不住的问："这是鸭子的哪个部位做的，我可以再吃一些吗？因为它真的很好吃"。鸭子的各个部位都有许多种吃法，你可能永远看不出来你吃的不同菜是同样的部位烹制而成。比如辣酱鸭肠、油炸鸭肠、青椒炒鸭肠等等。

The appetizing taste of duck can often make a foreigner forget rules of etiquette. An encounter with a roasted ducks head at the table is so appetizing you wish you were at home, in private, to take the head by your fingers, and crack it between your teeth. Eating a duck's head is supposed to bring good luck. Then there is a slight pause as the duck gizzard in a light broth circles the table to one's delight.

鸭肴的美味常常会让外国人在中国用餐时忘记餐桌礼仪。当你在餐桌邂逅鸭头，是如此令人垂涎欲滴，以至于你希望自己在家里，私下里用手拿住鸭头，咬破鸭头之间的骨头，因为吃鸭头据说能带来好运。然后稍事休息，会有清汤鸭胗呈上，让你回味无穷。

In Beijing and other Chinese cities duck is considered a sumptuous dish for the formal dining table and on official large festive social events. In Chinese cuisine and food groups the nutritional value of duck is rated similar or healthier than chicken. However, the exciting aspect of duck is that every part can be prepared as a single dish, including the feet. The presentation of duck feet is done in fine style at the meal table in Beijing and throughout China and it's fully included in formal dining.

在北京和中国其他城市，鸭肴总是被视为正式餐桌上和重大节庆社交活动上的丰盛佳肴。在中国菜肴中，鸭肴的营养价值与鸡肉相似甚至更健康。然而，令人兴奋的是，鸭的每个部位都可以单独制成一道菜，包括鸭掌。鸭掌在餐桌上总会以一种优雅的风格呈现，正餐中也会有它的身影。

A large variety of popular duck dishes are served, as you like it. Duck meat for its flavor is used as the main ingredient of many delicious dishes. Numerous dishes are conjured up including a foreigner's favorite, crispy duck, duck bone soup, fried duck pieces, fried duck with coriander and braised duck feet. I have not seen the feathers of the duck eaten, but I see dusters made with those feathers.

只要你喜欢，你可以尝到很多受欢迎的鸭肉菜肴，包括脆皮鸭、鸭架汤、炸鸭片、香菜炒鸭、红烧鸭掌。鸭毛还可以做成鸭毛掸子。

To watch a whole popular Peking duck getting sliced into pieces before your eyes is rather impressive; it is like watching an accomplished sculptor chip away; revealing his subject from beneath the pile of layers of rings of a huge tree trunk. The slices of duck are laid out on a platter and commonly eaten with thinly sliced fresh vegetables. The popular assortment of vegetables includes green onion, fresh cucumber and more with sweet soybean paste, wrapped in a pancake made from flour and water. Thinking about it makes my mouth water.

看着一整只北京烤鸭在你眼前被切成片状，确实令人印象深刻；这就像是看着一位技艺精湛的雕塑家不断削减，从巨大的树干环圈堆叠下露出他的作品。鸭肉片被摆放在一个盘子上，通常与薄切的新鲜蔬菜一起食用，常见的蔬菜组合包括青葱、新鲜黄瓜等，再蘸上甜面酱，用饼皮包裹送进嘴里；想一想都会让人垂涎欲滴。

There is plenty to learn, apart from eating duck. Gastronomy in China is an amazing feat. There are creative, innovative, and astonishing features of cuisine that reveal a most unique civilization.

When one ventures into an eating establishment that serves duck in Beijing, Hong Kong Nanjing or any other city or province in China; the pleasantries begin upon arrival. Much is revealed about the characteristics of Chinese citizens by the greetings upon arrival, which seems much more than ordinary restaurant hospitality. When one sits down to eat a Peking duck dish, the service becomes full of drama, and so entertaining, it teases the appetite. First, one is advised to reserve adequate time. When a whole duck is ordered, preparation cannot be rushed.

在中国还有很多东西需要学习。美食确实是一项惊人的壮举。中国菜的创造性令人惊叹，也显示出一种最独特的文明。

在北京、香港、南京或中国其他城市或省份，当人们进入烤鸭餐厅时，一到那里就开始寒暄起来。从抵达时的问候中可以看出中国人的特点，这似乎比在普通的餐厅更加热情。当人们坐下来吃北京烤鸭的时候，服务变得充满了戏剧性，而且非常有趣，挑逗着人们的胃口。如果是点了一整只鸭子，要预留足够的时间，准备工作是不可仓促进行的。

Duck is a considered a representative dish reflective of Chinese pride on a dining table and a special meal. The nutritious value of duck while similar in many ways to that of a chicken, its nutritional value is of higher quality than these poultry dishes. In modern Chinese cuisines duck is made ready for the table in an amazing variety of styles and palates.

在中国，鸭肴一直被视为餐桌上的代表性菜肴，反映了中国人的自豪感，是一道特别的餐点。尽管鸭肉在许多方面与母鸡或公鸡肉相似，但其营养价值被广泛认为更高质。中国菜肴里鸭肉总是能被做成令您眼花缭乱的菜品。

Is he a chef or a carver?
这是位厨师还是雕刻师呢？

Who ever thought that when the capital city Roast Duck was introduced in the Yuan Dynasty, there would be such proliferation of duck dishes throughout the People's Republic of China and throughout the global Chinese diaspora?

谁曾想到，当元代的京城烤鸭问世后，会有如此多的鸭肉菜肴在整个中华人民共和国和已走向世界的中国侨民中不断发展？

English	Chinese	Pronunciation	Characters
Beijing roast duck	Běijīng kǎoyā	bay-jing kaoww-yaa	北京烤鸭
Quanzhou ginger (female) duck	Quánzhōu jiāng mǔyā	chwen-joh jyang moo-yaa	泉州姜母鸭
Nanjing brine-boiled duck	Nánjīng yánshuǐ yā	nan-jing yen-shway yaa	南京盐水鸭
Hangzhou old duck soup	Hángzhōu lǎo yā bāo	hung-joh laoww yaa baoww	杭州老鸭煲
Shredded roast duck with jellyfish	fèi hǎizhē bàn huǒ yā sī	fay heye-jer ban hwor yaa srr	鸭丝拼海蜇
Duck tongues with assorted vegetables	tiáo cài bàn yā lì	tyaoww tseye ban yaa lee	鸭舌拼杂蔬
Duck wings with coriander	xiāngsuī yā yì	sshyang-sway yaa ee	香菜鸭翼
Fried duck tongues with tangerine peel	chénpí yā lì	chnn-pee yaa lee	陈皮鸭舌
Guilin "vinegar and duck blood" duck	Guìlín cù xuè yā	gway-lin tsoo sshwair yaa	桂林醋血鸭
Nine foot pressed salted duck	jiǔ chǐ bǎnyā	jyoh chrr ban-yaa	九尺板鸭
Gaoyou fried crispy duck	Gāoyóu xiāng sūmá yā	gaoww-yoh sshyang soo-ma yaa	高邮炸鸭
Hainan Barbary duck	Hǎinán jiājī yā	heye-nan jyaa-jee yaa	海南野鸭

Duck - Authentic Chinese Cuisine
正宗中国美食-鸭肉

As the Chinese culture circulates and the world encounters Peking roast duck, its appeal makes it famous and enjoyed in many communities. Wherever it is eaten, it retains the authenticity and characteristics of Chinese in preparation and serving.

随着中国文化的传播，世界各地的人们都可以品尝到北京烤鸭，它的吸引力使其在许多地方变得著名并备受喜爱。但无论在哪里供应，它都保留了在制备和呈现方面的中国特色。北京烤鸭是中国饮食文化的重要代表，无论是在中国还是国际社会上，它都是一道备受推崇的美食。

Did you know that in some parts of China, ducks are walked like dogs, and dogs are eaten? But let's not get distracted by dog meat. However, if you insist take a trip to Yulin, or Guangxi where annual festivals of eating Dog meat is held. But, while it may be a favorite of many, let's get to know more and find the secret of roast duck and China. They walk ducks in flocks to graze and water. They are kept in pens at night to keep them safe. Walking ducks causes huge traffic jams on occasions in some parts of China.

在中国的一些地方，你知道人们溜鸭子但吃狗肉吗？我们在此不提狗肉。但如果你坚持要去玉林或广西旅行，那里每年都会举行狗肉节。我们还是继续研究烤鸭的秘密吧。有人像牧牛一样放养鸭子，把鸭子赶到有牧草或者水域的地方，等到晚上把它们赶回圈舍以保证它们的安全，但是有时候放养鸭子也会造成交通拥堵。

A duck is a duck Ok; however, it must be made known, that there is wide variety of duck dishes. And did you know that there is a variety of duck the species? How many can you name, and which do you think taste the best?

我们知道有各种各样的鸭肉美食，但是鸭子种类繁多，你可以叫的上来的名字有多少呢，你认为哪种口味的鸭肉最好呢？

- A ring-necked duck 环颈鸭

- Peking duck 北京鸭

- North American wood duck 北美木鸭

- Mandarin duck 鸳鸯

- Khaki Campbell 康贝尔鸭

- Crested Swedish 凤头瑞典鸭

- Mallard duck 绿头鸭

- Indian Runner duck 印度跑鸭

- Blue Cayuga 蓝色卡尤加鸭

- Wild ducks 野鸭

There is the charmingly ugly Muscovy duck, there are farmed ducks, domesticated ducks, and more duck including perching, diving and dabbling ducks.

有憨态可掬的美洲家鸭，有养殖鸭，还有栖息鸭，潜水鸭，和钻水鸭。

Chapter 6
Taste of Authentic Chinese Cuisine
Duck in the Caribbean

第6章
在加勒比品尝正宗的中国鸭肴

We can't stop wondering why duck until the world gets to know about the Caribbean Chinese cooking of duck. To close this discussion about why duck, I invite you to discover the exciting duck dishes prepared by Caribbean Chinese, where Duck Curry is prepared in Guyana. There the duck is so good it makes you bite your hand. Let us begin with some history.

Caribbean Chinese cuisine is a popular style of food resulting from a blending of Chinese and West Indian or Caribbean cuisines. The Chinese influence, in the Caribbean, which is predominantly Cantonese, emerges from the Hakka, the main source of Chinese immigrants to the West Indies. This ethnic group of China was originally the Hakka from the North China. Research supports that they migrated to the South of China, especially Guangdong, Fujian, Jiangxi, and Guangxi provinces, during the fall of the Nan (Southern) Song dynasty in the 1270s. It is from these major groups of Chinese, spoken of as the Hakka people, came the people throughout southern China, Taiwan, Hong Kong and all over the Caribbean diaspora, and among overseas Chinese around the world.

Caribbean or West Indian food is itself a mixture of all the colonial experiences such as African, British, Indian, Spanish, French and Indigenous cooking panaches. Although it's a long-favored cuisine in West-Indian eating places, and Chinese-Caribbean households, it is only in modern times that an explosion in Caribbean-Chinese restaurants has surfaced.

在我不禁想为什么要吃鸭肉的时候，加勒比地区的华人对鸭肉的烹饪给了我答案。所以我也在此邀请大家一起探索加勒比地区华人烹制的令人兴奋的鸭肴，比如圭亚那的咖喱鸭，就非常好吃。

加勒比地区的中国菜是一种很流行的美食风格，由中国和西印度菜系混合而成。加勒比地区受中国影响主要来自广东，以客家人为主要中国移民源头。这个中国族群最初是来自中国北方的客家人，但研究显示他们在1270年代南宋灭亡期间迁移到中国南方，特别是广东、福建、江西和广西省。客家人在中国南部、台湾和香港以及整个加勒比海地区乃至世界各地聚居。

加勒比或西印度的饮食风格本身就是所有殖民饮食经验的混合，包括非洲、英国、印度、西班牙、法国和土著烹饪风格。尽管西印度餐馆和中国加勒比家庭中的饮食一直以来都比较受欢迎，但直到近年来，加勒比式中餐馆的才出现激增。

Dàzhǔ gānsī

Dàzhǔ gānsī is a typical soup dish of Huaiyang cuisine. It is made of finely sliced dried tofu, chicken, ham and bamboo shoots; ingredients braised with shrimp in chicken soup.

It was highly praised by the Qianlong emperor.

大煮干丝是淮扬菜的一道典型汤菜。它由切成细丝的豆腐干、鸡肉、火腿和竹笋制成，配料需要与鸡汤中的虾一起炖煮。它受到乾隆皇帝的高度赞扬。

Làzǐ Jī, stir-fried chicken with chili and Sichuan pepper in Sichuan style
川式辣椒炒鸡肉

Steamed whole perch
清蒸鲈鱼

Steamed whole perch with roe inside.
Sliced ginger and spring onion are usually spread on top.
清蒸整条鲈鱼，鱼内有鱼籽。
通常会撒上切成薄片的姜和葱段。

Because Chinese society greatly valued gastronomy, an extensive study was developed based on the subject and traditional medical beliefs. Chinese culture initially centered around the North China Plain. The first domesticated crops seem to have been the foxtail and broomcorn varieties of millet, while rice was cultivated in the south. By 2000 BC, wheat had arrived from western Asia. These grains were typically served as warm noodle soups instead of baked into bread as in Europe.

由于中国社会非常重视烹饪，因此基于这一主题和传统医学信仰进行了广泛研究。中国文化最初以华北平原为中心，最早开始种植的是狐尾草和高粱，而水稻是在南方种植的。到公元前2000年，小麦从西亚传入。这些谷物通常被制成温热的面汤，而不是像在欧洲那样被烤成面包。

Nobles hunted various wild game and consumed mutton, pork and dog as these animals were domesticated. Grain was stored against famine and flood and meat was preserved with salt, vinegar, curing, and fermenting. The flavor of the meat was enhanced by cooking it in animal fats though this practice was mostly restricted to the wealthy; By the time of Confucius in the late Zhou, gastronomy had become a high art. Confucius discussed the principles of dining: The rice husk must be meticulously removed, and the meat should be finely sliced. Refrain from consuming spoiled or rotten grains, fish, or meat. Reject unappetizingly colored or foul-smelling food. Abstain from poorly cooked dishes. Do not eat before the designated mealtime. Avoid poorly cut foods. Without the appropriate seasoning and condiments, abstain from eating. While an abundance of meat may be present, it should not surpass staple foods. Unlimited is the consumption of alcohol, but one should not drink to the point of losing consciousness. Do not partake in the consumption of market-bought wine and dried meat. After the meal, ginger need not be removed, but moderation is advised"

贵族狩猎各种野生动物，食用羊肉、猪肉和狗肉，因为这些动物已经被驯化。粮食被储存起来以防饥荒和洪水，而肉类则用盐、醋、腌制和发酵等方法保存。用动物脂肪烹饪肉类可以增强肉类的风味，但这种做法大多限于富裕阶层。到了周朝晚期的孔子时代，烹饪已经成为一门高超的艺术。孔子讨论了用餐的原则："食不厌精，脍不厌细。食饐而餲，鱼馁而肉败，不食；色恶，不食；臭恶，不食；失饪，不食；不时，不食；割不正，不食；不得其酱，不食。肉虽多，不使胜食气。唯酒无量，不及乱。沽酒市脯，不食。不撤姜食，不多食。"意即：粮食不嫌舂得精，鱼和肉不嫌切得细。粮食腐败发臭，鱼和肉腐烂，都不吃。食物颜色难看，不吃。气味难闻，不吃。烹调不当，不吃。不到该吃饭时，不吃。切割方式不得当的食物，不吃。没有一定的酱醋调料，不吃。席上的肉虽多，但不应超过主食。只有酒不限量，但不能喝到神志昏乱的地步。从市集上买来的酒和肉干，不吃。席毕，姜不撤除，但也不要多吃。

During Shi Huangdi's Qin dynasty, the empire expanded into the south. By the time of the Han dynasty, the different regions and cuisines of China's people were linked by major canals and leading to a greater complexity in the different regional cuisines. Not only is food seen as giving "qi", energy, but food is also about maintaining yin and yang. The philosophy behind it was rooted in the I Ching and Chinese traditional medicine: food was judged for color, aroma, taste, and texture. A good meal was expected to balance the Four Natures ('hot', warm, cool, and 'cold') and the Five Tastes (pungent, sweet, sour, bitter, and salty). Salt was used as a preservative from early times, but in cooking was added in the form of soy sauce, not at the table.

In Jamaica, one may encounter a Mr. David Lee and his celebrated Roast Duck a signature Jamaican Hakka dish, considered a must-have for any type of celebration dinner if you are from a Jamaican Chinese household. He does a Jamaican Chinese Style Roast Chicken, but we won't talk about that, because the introduction of Roast Duck Guyanese and Trinidad and Tobago Chinese elegance will woo you.

秦始皇初期，帝国向南方扩张。到了汉代，中国不同地区和人民的饮食被主要的运河连接起来，导致不同地区的饮食更加复杂。食物不仅被视为给予 "气"，即能量，而且食物还关系到维持阴阳。其背后的哲学植根于《易经》和中国传统医学：

判断食物的色、香、味、质，期望一顿好的食物能平衡四性（"热"、温、凉、"寒"）和五味（辛、甘、酸、苦、咸）。盐从早期就被用作防腐剂，但在烹饪中是以酱油的形式添加，而不会放在餐桌上。

在牙买加，你可能会遇到大卫·李先生和他做的有名的烤鸭，这是一道标志性的牙买加客家菜，通常是牙买加华人家庭各种活动的必备菜品。除此之外，他还做牙买加客家风味烤鸡，我们可以以后再探讨，再来看看圭亚那和特立尼达和多巴哥的华人做的烤鸭。

curry duck 咖喱鸭

roast duck烤鸭

How to make a delicious ultimate Guyanese Chinese duck, begins to reveal the creativity in Chinese culinary styles on the mainland that remains with the Chinese upon migration. It is therefore necessary that to taste a good Guyanese Chinese Duck, please contact the Embassy of Guyana if you are in China, or the most outstanding Ambassador Bayney Karran with whom I participated in duck dining while in China.

如何制作美味的圭亚那鸭也展示了中国烹饪风格的创意，这种风格在中国大陆上一直流传，也随着华人的迁徙传播到其他地方。如果你想品尝一道美味的圭亚那鸭又苦于不能前往圭亚那，那么在中国你可以联系圭亚那驻华大使馆，或者联系贝尼·卡伦大使，我曾与他一起在中国品尝过美味的鸭肴。

As a reminder when you taste Jamaican Chinese Style Roast Duck just call the Embassy of Jamaica when in China, you may be surprised and pleased to know that the ambassador's ancestral past takes him back to the south of China. When the research for this book was done, the Ambassador was Antonia Hughes. I asked him then how he compared Jamaican Chinese Style Roast Duck with Beijing's style He then told me how to contact Mr. Lee In Jamaica, for the recipe, and I will get part of the answer for "Why Duck".

如果你想要品尝牙买加中式烤鸭，可以打电话给牙买加驻华大使馆，你可能会惊讶的得知，大使的祖先就生活在中国南方。为这本书做研究时，我问牙买加大使安东尼亚·休，如何比较牙买加的中式烤鸭和北京烤鸭，他告诉我联系牙买加的李先生，或许可以找到配方。

Upon arriving in Trinidad & Tobago, one must remember that this Caribbean country has been named the "happiest" Caribbean country to live in, according to the United Nations (UN). Trinidad and Tobago was ranked 38th happiest country in the world based on the 2018 World Happiness Report released by the Sustainable Development Solutions Network for the United Nations. In Trinidad and Tobago, they cut up the duck, but Duck is served. In addition to Roast Duck, y o u c a n f i n d duck-kabobs, duck creole, duck gumbo, pan fried, deep fried, and stir-fried duck. There's pineapple duck, lemon duck, coconut duck, curry duck, duck soup, duck stew, duck salad, duck and potatoes, duck burger, duck sandwich. That is not all, but to know more, call the Embassy of Trinidad &Tobago in China, I know that there is an officer at that Embassy that could really cook well, and the Ambassador when I visited to discuss duck, in Trinidad and Tobago, spoke excellent Chinese.

根据 2018 年的数据显示，特立尼达和多巴哥，被联合国（UN）评为幸福指数最高的加勒比国家，世界排名第38位。在特立尼达和多巴哥，你可以找到烤鸭，鸭肉串，还有鸭肉浓汤，以及煎、炸、炒的鸭肉，菠萝鸭、柠檬鸭、椰子鸭、咖喱鸭、炖鸭、鸭肉沙拉、土豆鸭、鸭子汉堡、鸭子三明治。这还不是全部，如果想了解更多，可以联系特立尼达和多巴哥驻华大使馆，我知道该大使馆有一位外交官做得一手好鸭，大使的中文也很不错。

Have you ever had duck from Grenada? This is a well-kept secret you will have to visit Grenada for exclusive Roast Duck, because it's everywhere.

你品尝过格林纳达的鸭肉吗？这是一个不为人知的秘密，你必须前往格林纳达品尝独家的烤鸭，因为它随处可见。

The long history of duck dining eating, Kao Ya (roast duck) in Beijing is quite colorful.

Duck dining in Beijing

Kao ya is a world celebrated dish; and we can agree that almost every foreigner to visit China has tried this food. But do you still wonder why this dish is so attractive? What is the magic of roast duck? It could be the history of KAO YA. It started at the time of the southern and northern dynasties. In addition to the fact that the emperor Zhu Yuanzhang loved the way the duck was cooked using charcoal fire,the flavor was fantastic! That's where this dish was named 'kao ya'. At that time there were only two ways to cook duck in the tradition 'kao ya'; roast it or braise it.

北京烤鸭的历史绚烂多彩而又绵长悠久

烤鸭被公认为是世界著名菜肴。几乎每个外国人来中国都要品尝烤鸭。你是否还在想为什么烤鸭如此诱人？烤鸭的烹饪秘诀又是什么？这就需要回顾烤鸭的发展历史了。烤鸭起源于南北朝时期。明朝皇帝朱元璋非常喜欢用木炭生的火烤鸭子，其味道十分鲜美。这也是为什么人们称之为烤鸭的原因。那个时候鸭肉的烹饪只有两种方式，烤或者蒸。

Beijing duck in the oven
烤炉中的鸭子

Duck from the oven to the table in Beijing
上桌的烤鸭

Just imagine that centuries ago the first kao ya restaurant in Beijing called 'Bian yi fang' was opened. To this day, 'Bian yi fang' restaurants are found in Beijing. I wonder if they prepare Historic Duck instead of roast duck. Have you wondered how this folk culture and cooking tradition have stood the test of time into today's modern China? This historic duck meat preparation and its evolution are a true example that experience, and customs do not grow old but add value that can define people and shape societies. And here is where again the concepts of Chinese characteristics come to mind. I wonder if you would agree to add determination, adventure, and nationalism? These sentiments indicate a special kind of quiet humility driven by an inner passion to succeed.

想象几个世纪以前一个叫"便宜坊"的烤鸭店开张，到今天在北京仍可以找到。所以我在想他们是否在准备一只极具历史性的烤鸭而不是简单的烤鸭。你是否想知道这样的民俗文化和烹饪工艺是如何历经时间的考验而仍然活跃在现代中国的？烤鸭的历史和革新充分证明，风俗是不会变老的，只会不断增添价值，而这些价值却可以定义一个民族和社会。

I am always struck by the adulation in the voice when asked by a Chinese citizen 'do you like Chinese food?'. Therefore, why duck? Roast Duck is more than just an element of tradition in Chinese cuisine. Roast duck is as a main element in the diplomatic history of China. It was highlighted for its role during very significant negotiations. Roast duck on the table for lunch, could be credited to "help smooth over differences during the 1971 meeting between the former Secretary of State of the USA Henry Kissinger, and the late Premier Zhou Enlai. But more than that, it is culturally significant to note that the cooking techniques of duck have been on China's Intangible Cultural Heritage List since 2008. This is significant, as Intangible cultural heritage is considered by UNESCO in relation to the tangible World Heritage focusing on intangible aspects of culture. In 2001, UNESCO conducted a survey among States and non-governmental organizations to try to agree on a meaning. The Convention for the Safeguarding, protection and promotion of Intangible Cultural Heritage was put in place. Why Duck? This question is intended to entice one's curiosity about Chinese culture in foods and the observations of how foods and eating in China relate to and reveal values and customs when foreign eyes can see.

当中国人问我是否喜欢中国菜的时候，我总是被这问声中的自豪所打动。回顾在中国做大使的经历，我发现烤鸭不仅仅是中国菜肴中的一个传统元素，还是中国外交史上的一个主要元素。在非常重要的谈判中，它的作用会被不断强调。在 1971 年美国前国务卿基辛格和已故总理周恩来之间的会议上，烤鸭可以说是 "帮助平息了分歧"。不仅如此，自2008 年以来，鸭子的烹饪技术被列入中国的非物质文化遗产名录，这也是一种传承且意义重大，众所周知，教科文组织将非物质文化遗产与注重非物质文化方面的有形世界遗产相提并论。2001 年，联合国教科文组织在各国和非政府组织中进行了一次调查，试图就其含义达成一致，并制定了《关于保护、保存和促进非物质文化遗产的公约》。

为什么食鸭？这个问题旨在激发人们对饮食中的中国文化的好奇心，以及当外国人观察中国的饮食方式时，食物和用餐如何关联并展示出价值观和风俗习惯。

Chapter
7

Food in new era
第7章 新时代美食

I became interested in what young Chinese citizens have to say about Chinese cuisine and dining. During a chat with a young man who works in Beijing. I asked him about what comes to mind when he thinks about telling a foreigner about Chinese food. What surprised me was his introduction of Kao ya, when I told him I was interested in Kao ya. I soon learned about baked fish Chongqing. He quickly reminded me that when he was young his family was poor; they cooked potatoes. What are your childhood food memories? He said it was spicy food he ate which he will never forget. Until today he loves spicy foods. It was then I learned that young professionals in the major cities of China dine out. We never cook, my generation can't spend an hour to cook something, it's not worth the time; one hour work has more value than cooking. Cooking is not on the to-do list. The older age group in China cooks, but young people born in the late 1980's and 90's do not cook much at home anymore. When young people are single, they have no time to cook; that's consumer time. We are consumers, there is too much to do, and cooking is time lost. Imagine one works for 200 Renminbi per hour and spends 20 for a good meal. It is better to eat out because food is not expensive. But what do you think about the quality of the food? Well, not good; better to eat in the huge restaurants where the quality is better. Young people don't eat at small places. Time is very important for city dwellers, and to spend two hours cooking and eat for 30 minutes is not for China today. It is almost like speed eating because there is only two hours for lunch break. It would be better to eat and take a walk. Our generation Millennia Sam responded, are fast eaters. We must win the market once you have the market more money. Now spicy food is it for the young generation, it is as if it stimulates us. Spicy foods are taking over. Hot pot is growing. I believe that the younger generation does not have the art of cooking like their parents. Well since you have travelled what about eating when you travel. Well, the foods abroad are not Chinese food even if a Chinese national cooks when out of China they cannot train cooks in true the art of Chinese cooking, to cook Chinese food as is done in China. Cooks in China have higher standards.

我对中国年轻人对中国美食的看法非常感兴趣。我与一位在北京工作的年轻一代中国人进行了非常有趣的讨论。我问他，要向外国人介绍中国菜的时候，他会选哪一道菜。

当我告诉他我对烤鸭感兴趣时，他给我介绍了烤鱼。我很快就了解了重庆烤鱼。他跟我说，在他很小的时候，他家很穷，总是煮土豆。我问他，童年的食物记忆是什么，他说他吃的都是辛辣的食物，而且直到今天，他仍然喜欢辛辣的食物。

这时我才知道，中国大城市的很多年轻人常在外面吃饭。他们从不做饭，他说我们这一代人不可能花一个小时去做饭，这不值得花时间，一个小时的工作比做饭更有价值。做饭不在待办事项之列。 在中国，年龄较大的群体会做饭，但80年代末和90年代出生的年轻人在家里不怎么做饭。年轻人单身时，没有时间做饭，做饭太浪费时间。想象一下，一个人每小时可以赚200元，花20元就可以吃一顿饭，还是在外面吃划算。我问他食物的质量如何？他说不怎么样。最好是在大餐厅吃饭，好吃也干净。时间对他们来说非常重要，花两个小时做饭，吃30分钟，这不适合今天的中国。因为只有两个小时的午休时间，还不如边吃边走。他说他们这一代人是速食者，他们必须赢得市场，一旦有了市场就会赚更多的钱。年轻一代喜欢吃辣，辣味食品正在占领市场，火锅不断兴起。年轻一代没有像他们的父母那样掌握烹饪的技艺。我接着问他，既然你出国留学了，那么在国外的饮食情况如何呢？他说国外菜与中国菜大不相同，即使是中国人做的，也不如中国本土菜正宗，国外的厨师没有受过中国烹饪培训，没有按照中国人的口味和做法来做中国菜。

It is important to take note that in China we eat everything. One very interesting food I would like to tell foreigners about, and that is Mapo Tu fu, once you eat it you can't forget it. I encourage foreigners visiting China to be open-minded. Foreigners miss too much when they are scared about what to eat; because there is no other nation in the world like us. What about poverty in China? Well, there is poverty in places because of the geography, the land for farming is not done there. Are young people concerned about healthy eating? Well, we all know there is a lot of chemicals growing and preparing the foods but right now we can't do anything about that. There is one other food all foreigners should try and that is the emperor's meal Manhan quanxi; this is a combination of many dishes.

他接着说："在中国我们吃的东西非常多样。我想告诉外国人一种非常有趣的食物，那就是麻婆豆腐，一旦你尝过一次，就再也无法忘记。我鼓励来中国的外国人要有开放的心态。当外国人害怕吃有些东西的时候，实际就会错过很多东西。"我问他："中国的贫困情况如何？"他说："有些地方很贫穷，因为地理原因，那里的土地不适合耕种。""年轻人关注健康饮食吗？""我们都知道有很多化学制品添加，但现在我们对此无能为力。 还有一种食物是所有外国人都应该尝试的，那就是满汉全席。

There is much talk about Yulin. I understand that, but foreigners need to be opened minded as mentioned before. Dog Meat Festival, which took place around the summer, is not as popular as it used to be.

For the young Chinese professional, it seems obvious there is belief in families of reference to the relevance of remembering the relationship of the five natural elements and our foods. Teaching within families about food refers to gold and water, fire, wood, and land, and how these elements relate to what we eat. I was surprised to hear that young people in China think that the quality of the foods could be better managed. Profit is what it is about, and while there is growing confidence in the food establishments, the standards differ a lot.

关于玉林的话题很多。我对此表示理解，但如前所述，外国人需要有开放的心态。夏天前后举办的狗肉节已经不像以前那么受欢迎了。关于中国年轻专业人士的信仰，似乎很明显的是，他们相信在家庭中，教导人们在食物中要记住自然五行与食物的关系。他们提到金、木、水、火、土，以及这些元素与我们所吃的东西的关系。我很惊讶地听到，中国的年轻人认为食品质量可以得到更好的管理。利润就是一切，虽然人们对食品企业越来越有信心，但标准却相差甚远。

Trade in food is complex. It requires careful analysis and interpretation, and trade in foodstuff is one of the largest volumes of trade China has with many countries. Upon entering retail food establishments, it is mind boggling to encounter the complexity of the variety of colorful displays of wrapped foods, canned foods, preserved, fermented, and biologically conserved items. There are too many to count and they range from the smallest items to huge group servings. There is no description for what may be found. There is dried preserved, roasted, and raw.

食品贸易是复杂的，需要仔细分析和解释，食品贸易是中国与许多国家最大的贸易之一。在进入食品零售场所时，你会看到各种五颜六色的包装食品、罐头食品、腌制食品、发酵食品等，种类多到数不清。

The art of processing and preservation of agricultural products reflects the application of technology into food production and preparation. However, reflecting on the duck here, which depicts centuries of proven trust in the method of roasting, what we can take away is the fact that there is persistence in Chinese ways. This persistence has paid off in providing adequate nutritious foods to move hundreds of millions out of poverty. Consumption of these modern packaged foods is a vibrant economic stimulus particularly among the younger citizens who think eating out is the way to go, if you are not married and even married couples agree cooking at home, while living in the city, is not economical because of the value placed on time.

农产品的加工和保存技术很好地反映了技术在食品生产和制备中的应用。烤鸭的悠久历史反映了几个世纪以来中国人对这种烤肉方法的信心，也反映了中国人处事的持之以恒。这种坚持也得到了回报，人们有了充足的营养食品，数亿人摆脱了贫困。在中国，这些现代包装食品的消费是最有活力的经济刺激方式，特别是在年轻的中国人中，如果他们没有结婚，在外面吃饭是一种常态，尽管有的已婚夫妇愿意在家里做饭，但生活在城市，因为对时间的重视，也会选择在外面吃，自己在家做不划算。

At the beginning of relationships, food is considered as an entry point for people to reach each other when in unfamiliar societies. Food is certainly a medium for building cultural bridges; and restaurants and eating situations, whether it is picnic, brown bag meals, potluck or formal dining, people are at their best in these situations.

在人际关系建立之初，食物被认为是人们在陌生社会中相互接触的切入点。现在，人们已经清楚地认识到，食物无疑是搭建文化桥梁的媒介；在餐厅和用餐环境中，无论是野餐，聚餐还是正式用餐，人们在这些环境中的表现都是最好的。

Sustenance food, food to meet the urgency in the fight against poverty, has become a highlight in the drive to eradicate abject poverty in China. It has become obvious that there is a global consciousness that China is moving ahead very fast and is bent on leaving no one behind. It is not just about feeding the population, but also keeping the society pleased and smiling, and with that, comes growing consumption and rising productivity. However, there is a growing concern expressed by health and wellness professionals, and families, concerning the impact on the younger generation. Among these disquiets is increased obesity in the youths, which is beginning to surface.

在中国消除贫困的行动中，获得维持生计的食物已经成为行动中的重点。中国正在快速向前发展，不甘落后于任何人。 这不仅仅是为了养活其人口，也是为了保持其社会的稳定与和谐，消费的增长和生产力的提高也随之而来。但是目前健康和保健专业人士对年轻一代表现出了担忧，因为青少年肥胖症开始浮现。

How is access to food contributing to the health anxieties, particularly among the policy makers and leaders?

食物的获取是如何加剧人们，尤其是决策者和领导者的健康焦虑的？

As a foreigner, it is impressive to observe the various calls to action and the health initiatives in China to raise awareness about health, not just health of those who can gain access to care, but to inform and educate the people. It was a remarkable experience when I was invited to make a presentation at a forum called the Launch of Healthy China 2030 program. This event brought together provincial city and community policy implementers to discuss, among other topics, the effective management and maintenance of quality in food production, preparation, and responsible representation of quality.

作为一个外国人，我观察到中国已经开始的各种呼吁行动和健康倡议令人印象深刻， 这些行动旨在提高人们对健康的认识，不仅仅是为那些能够获得医疗服务的人的健 康考虑，也是对人民的宣传和教育。我记得被邀请在一个名为 "健康中国 2030 计划启动仪式 "的论坛上做演讲。 这次活动聚集了省级城市和社区的政策执行者，讨论了如何有效管理和维护食品在生产制备中的质量问题。

Recalling the launch of Healthy China 2030, I began to focus on food in a hurry "Fast Food," and whether the culture of being on time for work has anything to do with the quality of fast foods, or whether the preparation of such lavish variety of foodstuffs has anything to do with the impact on health of fast foods. As a foreigner, I observe that there is a culture of food when you must get there, and the speed of consumption may have to be assessed for its impact on health. Nonetheless, one must begin to think about affluence and access to such a wide variety of imported foods on the physiology of the Chinese consumer.

Observing the way Chinese people have a meal and the way they are with each other during mealtime, also provides foreign eyes with a deep insight into their values. What can be observed about Chinese chefs, and cooking, is rather endearing. In general, the preparation and consumption of foods revel self-pride as one significant trait. There is a noticeable desire to please, therefore creating customer satisfaction with a large measure of desire for adulation; but of course, to boost the bottom line and demonstrate confidence in their art of cooking and serving.

回顾 "健康中国 2030 "的启动，我开始关注"快餐"，思考要求人们准时到岗工作是否与快餐的质量有关，或者快速准备多种多样的食品是否与快餐对健康的影响有关。作为一个外国人，我认为，可能必须评估消费的速度对健康的影响，考虑获得如此广泛的进口食品对中国消费者身体造成的影响。

观察中国人的用餐方式以及他们在用餐时的相处方式，也让外国人对中国的价值观有深刻的了解。中国厨师是极具耐心的，他们烹饪的菜品可以提高顾客满意度，同时他们也会得到顾客极大的称赞，这也是出于对他们的烹饪技术和服务的信心。

Although fast food preparation and service, appear to be eroding courtesies and caring; one can observe in certain cases of serving at fast foods establishments, a lot of no-look passing of dishes to customers, which can be considered very uncharacteristic of Chinese mealtime courtesies.

There are examples of dishes prepared in China that makes one wonder whether the foods eaten in can be adopted in other cultures and have the same impact, unlike Chinese roast duck, which has gone universal.

The taste of a country's food can create curiosity about wanting to know more about the origin of the food or the country from which it came. Such awareness has stirred up an interest to travel and visit various countries. Today there are many examples of food critics, or food explorers, traveling to "Parts Unknown" which have become popular television show in the USA and other developed countries that encourage viewers to indulge in, and explore the food cultures of a particular region, or country.

A culinary journey in China will take one very far, because China is no small village. As one travels through this vast civilization, one encounters many historic revelations of the survival of this once ancient, now modern civilization. There is astonishing disclosure of generating foods from sources unimaginable yet credible and affirmed as being at the foundation of producing foods through the ages.

快餐的准备和服务似乎正在侵蚀礼节和关怀；人们可以观察到在快餐店的某些情况下，很多人不经意地将菜肴递给顾客，这可以说是非常不符合中国用餐时间的礼节。

有一些中国菜的备制和服务也让人思考其他文化是否可以借鉴。食物的味道可以激起人们的好奇心，让人想知道食物的来源。这种意识激起了人们对旅行和参观不同国家的兴趣。如今，有许多美食评论家或美食探险家前往 "未知地区 "，这已成为美国一个流行的电视节目，鼓励观众探索某一特定地区或国家的饮食文化。

中国很大，在中国的美食之旅会让人走得很远。当人们在浩瀚的中国文明中行走时，中国古老文明的存续及其向现代文明的转变会给人许多历史性的启示。从难以想象但却可信的来源中产生的食物，可以被认定为是中国历代生产食物的基础。

Travelling through and discovering the taste of China, it was not much of a surprise to me that some of the ingredients are uncommon in many of the other countries I have visited.

Foods in China play a major part in all cultural festivals and family celebrations, as in most other countries.

From my experience as a witness and observer of the way Chinese citizens are with each other and their foods, in all settings, particularly during meals time; it is such a pleasant sight to behold the reverence and gratefulness that emanate. This makes me believe that such characteristics of a people that seem to reveal contentment makes China blessed.

Differentiating between local foods, imported foods and locally produced foods from imports is also an interesting experience. Among certain sectors of the populations there is a strong and growing interest in trying new or imported foodstuffs, with emphasis on quality.

Remember that the word quality, as a factor in the new era in China, holds great significance. Excellence and standard, if there is one thing to be said about roast duck it has stood the test of time. In my opinion, it is an imprimatur of quality for service, taste, and styles of presentation. Such tradition has retained its core attribute and its intangible secrets. Therefore, here I project endurance as a Chinese characteristic revealed in maintaining the standard of a tradition and culture.

在中国旅行，发现中国味道，这在我旅行过的许多其他国家中并不常见。与全球大多数其他国家一样，中国的食物在所有的文化节日和家庭庆祝活动中发挥着重要作用；在中国，我见证了中国人在各种场合下的就餐情形，可以感受到饭局间散发出来的崇敬和感激之情，这让我相信，是中国人对民族的满足感让中国得天庇佑。

区分本地食品、进口食品和本地生产的进口食品，在中国也是一个有趣的经历。有些人对尝试新食品或进口食品有强烈的兴趣，而且这种兴趣还在不断增长，他们比较注重食品的质量。质量在新时代的中国具有重大的意义，要求和标准。正如烤鸭，它经受住了时间的考验，在我看来，它是中国的口味和服务的质量印记。这种传统保留了它的核心属性和秘密性。我觉得这是中国人的耐力和坚持才使得中国的传统文化历久弥新。

The world has much to say about the food revolution in China and the success in feeding its population. The accomplishment has been cited for the valuable lessons to developing countries worldwide. Having lived and worked in China I prefer to call food in China more as a phenomenon rather than a revolution. My reason is because there is so much creativity and confidence that go into food. As mentioned earlier, there is also caring in eating.

The determination shared by China further unveils characteristics of a people, which provide lessons for leaders and policymakers across the developing world.

中国的粮食革命和中国在养活人口方面的成功为全世界的发展中国家提供了宝贵的经验。在中国生活和工作过的我更愿意把这称为一种现象而不是一场革命。因为在中国，人们在食物里注入了很多创造力，信心，和关怀。

中国的决心进一步揭示了其民族特点，为整个发展中国家的领导人和政策制定者提供了经验。

Chapter 8
Unique Chinese tastes to know in the USA.

第8章 在美国了解中国味道

I had the special privilege of sitting and dining at some establishments you may wish to visit. Be prepared because these dishes are appealing. Your taste and appetite may bring you back to that table more again and again.

我曾有幸在一些餐厅就餐，你也许会想去看看，但一定要做好准备，因为那里的菜肴非常诱人，可能会让你流连忘返。

On a visit to Atlanta in response to an invitation from my good friend Ambassador Dr. David Wu, I encountered the charm of Green Ocean that I can't forget. There I met Jane and her mom. I remember the irresistible Buddha Jumps Over the Wall Soup, which is also knows as Buddha's Temptation Soup.

The history of this soup is celebrated at Green Ocean, as depicted in this historic photograph about this dish that has maintained its place in China and its diaspora for over 150 years.

应好友大使吴大卫博士的邀请，我来到亚特兰大，邂逅了让我难以忘怀的绿海餐厅。在那里，我遇到了简和她的妈妈，吃到了让人难以抗拒的菜-佛跳墙。绿海餐厅对这道菜的历史进行了颂扬，正如这张照片所揭示的那样，这道菜在一个半世纪以来一直在中国保持着它的地位。

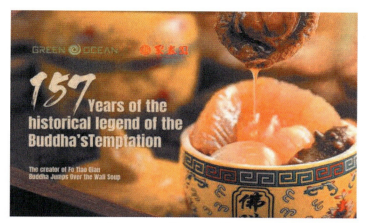

**Photos from Green
Ocean Atlanta**

Whenever you visit Atlanta, try Green Ocean Foods. What awaits on 5145 Buford Highway, in Doraville GA, 30340, is that soup, that golden broth, that can entice you to jump for who knows what; be careful when the taste tickles your pallet you must manage yourself.

The ingredients come direct from China, as Green Ocean imports and distributes with the USA ingredients that reveal the authentic taste of Chinese cooking.

因此，无论您何时来到亚特兰大，我都建议您品尝一下绿海餐厅的菜肴。在佐治亚州多拉维布福德公路 5145 号，等待您的就是那一碗汤，那一碗金黄色的汤，它能引诱您跳起来不知道要干什么，所以当您的味蕾被它刺激时，一定要小心，必须要淡定。

绿海餐厅总是提醒顾客，菜肴中的食材来自中国，这些食材展现了中国烹饪的正宗风味。

Photo of Green Ocean Showcase in Atlanta

The Washington, DC Metropolitan Area comprises a demographic with a vibrant appetite for Chinese culture and dining. This area is a center of community activities in the Chinese diaspora. Hence, there is growing awareness of popular Chinese American dining facilities and cultural facilities.

华盛顿特区大都会地区涵盖了对中国文化和饮食充满兴趣的人群。该地区是华人社区活动的中心，因此这里的人对受欢迎的中式美食的认知也在不断增强。

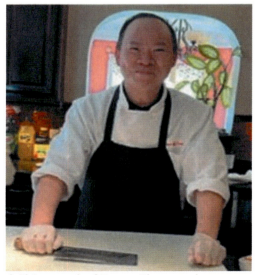
Meet famed Chinese chef Peter Chang - the man at the helm.
著名中国厨师彼得-张（Peter Chang）就是餐厅的掌舵人。

Peter Zhang is more than an authentic chef; he stands like a conductor of the culinary arts in the kitchen and in the dining establishments. Like an instrumentalist, he wheels the utensils and shuffles the ingredients that aggravate all the senses when dining at the table inspired by the masters of dynasties past as he prepares a lavish spread.

彼得·张不仅仅是一位地道的厨师，他在厨房和餐厅里就像一位烹饪艺术的指挥家，也像一位乐器演奏家，在餐桌上转动器皿，摆弄食材，让人在用餐时所有感官都受到历朝历代大师的启发。

I can tell you what I know but meeting Peter Zhang as I did will provide you with an in- person experience and your own understanding of the man and his craft. Begin with a visit at 4500 E West Highway, 100, in Bethesda, MD 20814 or the location most convenient to you. I do not call this humble man Chef but a Cultural Icon. Watching him work, he reflects the disposition of an artist and a conductor as he amusingly brings together the ingredients that inform the culinary process, which produces palatable dishes with his genus. His disposition translates his love of the art and secrets of food preparation that appeals to all the senses.

我可以告诉你我所知道的一切，但与彼得·张的会面将为你提供切身体验，让你了解这个人和他的手艺。您可以先去位于马里兰州贝塞斯达市4500 E 100 号参观，或者去离您近的分店也可以。他为人谦逊，我不称他厨师，而是文化偶像。他在餐厅工作的样子，体现出了艺术家和指挥家的气质，他风趣地将各种食材融合在一起，烹饪制作出美味的菜肴。他的性情也体现了他对中国烹饪艺术的热爱。

The growing appetite for the taste of China has inspired the following locations where one can be seduced by the sauces and the mouthwatering and eye-catching allure of Peters presentations. Be warned, it is possible to forget oneself thinking it's your personal space and have you linger. When you are visiting Washington, DC , Maryland, and Virginia, the following venues are highly recommended.

你可以去体验以下这些彼得·张的餐厅，相信你一定会被那些美味酱料以及令人垂涎的菜肴而吸引，品尝完说不定都不愿意离开。但当你访问华盛顿特区，马 里 兰 州 和 弗 吉 尼 亚 州 时 ， 强 烈 推 荐 以 下 场 所 ：

1. Peter Chang (Columbia) 6000 Merriweather Dr Suite B 175, Columbia, MD 21044 | (410) 413-5888) | (410)413-5887)

2. Q by Peter Chang (Bethesda)
   4500 East-West Hwy #100, Bethesda, MD 20814 | (240) 800-372

3. Chang Chang (DC)
   1200 19th St NW ste 110, Washington, DC 20036 | (202) 570-0946

4. NiHao (Baltimore)

   2322 Boston Street, Baltimore, MD 21224 | (443) 502-0597

(Photo with the permission of Permission of Peter Zhang)

5. Mama Chang (Fairfax)
   3251 Old Lee Hwy, Fairfax, VA 22030 | (703) 268-5556

6. Lu Wei by Peter Zhang (Fairfax)
   10728 Fairfax Blvd, Fairfax, VA 22030 | (571) 616-9988

7. Dim Sum by Peter Chang (Baltimore)
   1923 Ashland Ave, Baltimore, MD 21015 | (443) 888-3688

Chapter 9
Planting, growing, preparing, and marketing food in China.
第9章 在中国，食物的种植、培育、制备和销售

In China cooking a good dish seems to start with knowing where to find the right farms, the right produce, and the right ingredients. It is even significant to take note of how the food is grown, harvested, prepared, and presented in the marketplace. The display and promotion of foods have a lot to do with how the items retain their freshness and desired appearance from the field to the table. One must know where to find and buy the most authentic ingredients.

In farmers marketplaces, the combinations and varieties of foods are staggering. The volume of food is grand and the selection of items from which to choose is so diverse that one must have a good eye for the products to walk away with the best buyers.

The cut of pork or the quality of the fish or ground provisions selected may well determine the quality of the dish brought to the table.

Entering the marketplace to purchase the produce and the spice from such elaborate displays is an exercise that provides insights into the cultural knowledge of the buyers by the way they shop and make appropriate selections of raw produce in anticipation of unforgettable dishes.

在中国，要想烹饪一道美味的菜肴要知道在哪里能找到最好的食材。食物的陈列和售卖也要知道如何保持其新鲜度。

在中国的农贸市场，食材的品种多得让人眼花缭乱，所以必须要有敏锐的眼光，才能选购到最佳的食材。

猪肉的切割方式或鱼的新鲜度等，可能都会决定摆在餐桌上的菜肴的质量。走进市场，从如此复杂的陈列中挑选出合适的食材和配料，体现了买家对烹饪文化的知识储备，他们的选择也预示着能否做出一道让人印象深刻的菜肴。

**Display of vegetables, beans, ginger, and more in public marketplace in Beijing 2017
A corner store with vegetables, seasonings and kitchen items.**
2017年北京的市场上售卖的各种蔬菜、豆类、姜等
一个街边小商店里摆放着蔬菜、调味料和厨房用品

**Roadside market of roots, nuts, authentic spices, legumes and pods that conceal the
taste released in the right proportion by a skilled cook**

路边市场上摆放着根茎、坚果、地道香料、豆类和荚果，这些调料能够被熟练的
厨师以合适的比例展现出它们的独特味道

There is no shortage of meats in the markets with ready butchers.
市场上肉类充足，有熟练的屠夫随时为您服务

Knowing where to shop for the best foods is important. Some refreshing fruit juices can be purchased at this roadside market to combat the summer heat.

在中国，知道在哪里购买最好的食物同样重要，在这个路边市场可以买到一些清爽的果汁，以对抗夏季的炎热。

Making the right selection of produce from the farmers market is a first good step toward a great dish.

从农贸市场正确选择农产品是制作美味佳肴的第一步。

Sources of food include traditional farming and modern scientific methods such as hydroponics and aquaponics.

食物的来源：传统农业和现代科学方法，如水培和水草共生

There is a heavy demand for farm fresh vegetables, i n c l u d i n g cabbage, bok choy, potatoes, cucumbers and white radish.

对新鲜农产品包括卷心菜、白菜、土豆、黄瓜和白萝卜等需求很大

Farmers are the guarantors of the food revolution; they are reliable and show pride in their work.

农民是中国食品革命中的主要利益相关者，他们是食品革命的守护者，值得信赖并为自己的工作感到自豪。

Do you know what's coming to the table? This dish could be an adventure and a quail delight. Do our eating choices define us?

你知道桌上会上什么菜吗？这道菜可能是一场冒险，也可能是一场鹌鹑美馔。我们的饮食选择是否定义了我们呢？

Foreigners are cautioned to tread carefully when choosing from a traditional restaurant menu. The salted burning snail and steamed frog make an unforgettable adventure in eating.

外国人在点菜时要小心谨慎，腌制过的烧焗牛和蒸煮蛙会让用餐成为一次难忘的冒险

While dining in China there is an unmistakable presence of eggs in many tasty dishes. Fresh eggs are abundantly produced and on sale everywhere.

在中国用餐时，许多美味的菜肴都含有鸡蛋。新鲜鸡蛋随处可见，供应充足。

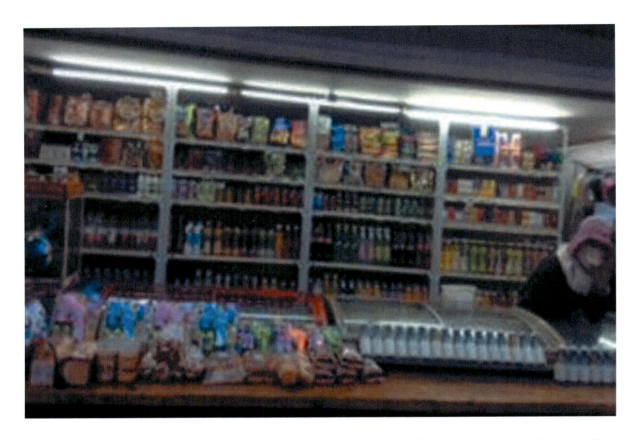

Authentic seasonings and spices are the signature of Chinese cuisine; without the right seasoning you are without a Chinese dish, The growers and distributors are fully aware and make them available in a variety of forms – bottles, jars boxes and bags, liquid and powdered.

正宗的调味品和香料是中国烹饪的招牌；没有合适的调料，就没有正宗的中国菜。种植者和经销商充分了解这一点，以各种形式提供调料——瓶装、罐装、盒装和袋装，液体和粉状。

The Dalian Haibao Fishery C0., Ltd. has many types of fish and crustaceans. Fish farming is a major aspect of the food industry. 大连海宝渔业有限公司提供多种多样的鱼和贝类。养殖业是食品工业的一个重要方面。

Modern farming includes a wide variety of crustaceans; however, shrimp, lobster and crabs remain popular on the menu.

现代养殖业包括多种贝类养殖，但在我们通常看到的菜单上，虾、龙虾和螃蟹仍然备受欢迎。

Photo taken at the Maotai Museum in southwest China's Guizhou province

在中国西南部的贵州省茅台博物馆拍摄的照片

A great meal is not complete without a generous toast with the favorite liquors such as the famous Moutai. (Photo taken at Moutai Museum)

一顿美餐离不开美酒，比如著名的茅台。 （照片摄于茅台博物馆）

There is always a celebration highlighted by a grand toast with liquor from all over the world. The stock of wines sometimes showcases the long history of brews. There is liquor that showcases Chinese wisdom, and liquor that inspires heroic spirit as described below.

每次庆祝活动都会由世界各地的美酒构成盛大的祝酒仪式。酒窖中的葡萄酒库有些展示了悠久的酿造历史。有些酒展示了中国的智慧，还有一些酒激发了人们豪迈的特性。

The hostess of the tea ceremony awaits with the most welcoming disposition extended to all, in a joyful manner showing her pleasure to serve.

茶艺表演的女主持人热情的迎接所有人，以欢快的方式展示着她乐于服务的高兴心情。

Beverages, hot and cold, have a special place in the food and hospitality traditions. From the spectacular fields of tea of Guizhou, one of the most breathtaking provinces in China, and the home of more than 16 distinct groups of ethnic minority people,he tea ceremony is luxurious. The fascinating local cultural festivals filled with special dishes and spirits liven up the moods of all in attendance. The pleasantries exhibited can only be explained through one's own experience.

无论是冷饮还是热饮，在中国的饮食传统中都占有特殊地位。在有16个少数民族的中国贵州，这里的广阔茶园令人叹为观止。茶道就像当地文化节日一样热闹讲究。

　　这些文化节日中有特色的菜肴和饮品，可以让所有参与其中的人的情绪变得更加活跃，这种氛围要亲自体验才能理解。

Welcome to the family fish restaurant in Dalian where you can get special Iron pot stewed fish, fish flavored shredded pork over rice and other dishes.

欢迎光临大连的农家鱼馆，这里提供特色的铁锅炖鱼、鱼香肉丝盖饭等美味佳肴。

Working, dining, and living in China?

在中国的工作，饮食和生活

It is intended that this book answers the question 'why duck' and generates a deeper understanding about meeting people where they are comfortable, in their own cultural space; and where they are engaged in their customs within their natural environments. My observations are that people who meet people, and take time to observe and interact, come away with realizing human similarities that are generally overlooked because of learned stereotypes.

这本书的目的是回答"为什么食鸭"这个问题，以及更深入地了解如何与不同的人在其舒适的文化空间中相遇，以及在他们成长的自然环境中参与了解他们的习俗。我的观察结论是，与人交往并花时间观察和与其互动，更容易发现因为刻板印象而被忽视的人类共通之处。

A frequent question I am asked is, what is it like working and living in China? I have always tried to answer after careful reflection. Living in China is quite a complex set of experiences, considering that I was born and grew up in the small island of Grenada. I find that there is plenty of space and people in China. It is in China that I have seen the largest number of persons in one open area. It is in China that I have seen the biggest buildings, the longest trains, and the longest bridge.

经常有人问我，在中国工作和生活是什么感觉？我总是尽力经过仔细思考后回答。生活在中国是一系列相当复杂的经历，考虑到我出生并在格林纳达小岛长大。我发现中国有我不曾见过的众多地方和人。中国是我见过在一个开阔区域范围内人数最多的地方。在中国，我见过最大的建筑物和最长的火车以及最长的桥梁

It is also in China that I have seen the largest group of people dining together in pleasant silence with an enjoyable look on their faces. It is in China that I have seen the widest variety of foods, and it's there that I have seen the most orderly movement of people going in and out of crowded entrances and exits. It is in China that I see order and patience on the longest lines for services of all categories.

在中国，我还看到过共进晚餐人数最多的场景，他们围坐在一起，人人脸上洋溢着笑容。在中国，我见过最丰富多样的美食，也看到人们在拥挤的入口和出口之间有条不紊地进出。在中国，我看到各类服务中人们排着长队，很有秩序，也很有耐心。

Living in the big cities of China one encounters well-coordinated cultural expressions with carefully planned pageants choreographed with synchronized patterns of movements. And music and colorful flowers and symmetrical designs that contribute to making the environment peaceful.

在中国的大城市生活，人们会遇到精心策划的各中文化表达方式，包括别具一格的庆典，有着各种一致动作的编排。还有音乐、五彩斑斓的花朵和对称的设计，这些元素共同营造了一种和谐的氛围。

I have learned to appreciate the leisure pursuit exposed in a sort of dutiful expression of acknowledgement of the amenities of life, by the energy exerted to reflect pride in the pleasures of life. The frequency and respectful toasting of persons at a feast appreciating their individual achievement or value as a person, I find to be admirable Chinese characteristic of celebration and respect for one another.

通过在生活中点滴付出的精力，我体会到了生活中的愉悦和自豪感，并且学会了欣赏对休闲生活的追求。在宴会上，我看到人们频繁而充满敬意地举杯致意，以表达对彼此个人成就或价值的欣赏，我觉得这是中国人在庆祝中表达敬意的一种令人钦佩的特征。

To order additional copies of this book, contact:
Xlibris
844-714-8691
www.Xlibris.com
Orders@Xlibris.com

ISBN: 979-8-3694-0692-2 (sc)
ISBN: 979-8-3694-0691-5 (e)

Library of Congress Control Number: 2023916866

Print information available on the last page

Rev. date: 01/17/2024

Xlibris
844-714-8691 www.Xlibris.com

ISBN：平装本 979-8-3694-0692-2
电子书 979-8-3694-0691-5

美国国会图书馆控制号：2023916866

修订日期：2023 年 12 月 01 日

Printed in the United States
by Baker & Taylor Publisher Services